MW00698812

Evolutionary Education

Moving Beyond Our Competitive Compulsion

Brent Zeller

WingSpan Press

Printed in the United States of America

Published by WingSpan Press, Livermore, CA
www.wingspanpress.com

The WingSpan name, logo and colophon are the trademarks of
WingSpan Publishing.

First edition 2009

Editors: Nancy Grimley Carleton & Doug Childers
Editorial Assistance: David Blake & Michael Katz
Cover Art: Alan Babbitt & Omar Ramirez

Lyrics to Grateful Dead songs by Robert Hunter and John Barlow,
copyright Ice Nine Publishing Company. Used with Permission.

Publisher's Cataloging-in-Publication Data
Zeller, Brent.
Evolutionary education : moving beyond our competitive compulsion
/ Brent Zeller.
p. cm.
ISBN: 978-1-59594-309-5
1. Teaching. 2. Competition (Psychology). 3. Learning. I. Title.
LB1025.3 Z452 2009
371.102`01—dc22   2009927350

*This book is dedicated to the multitudes that have
suffered the negative effects of a competitive system,
and to the brighter future which is possible from
an excellence based, non-competitive learning system.*

A mind once stretched by a new idea never regains its original dimension.

— Oliver Wendell Holmes

Contents

Preface

It's all a dream we dreamed
One afternoon long ago
— Robert Hunter

In 1988, after twenty years of learning and playing the sport of tennis, and 14 years of teaching it, I had a simple realization: The introduction of competition before we achieve proficiency in the fundamental physical, mental and emotional skills, compromises all aspects of the learning process. Unfortunately, this premature introduction of competition into the learning process occurs not just in tennis and other sports, but in almost every field of skill and knowledge in our culture. And the consequences for individuals and society are devastating. Today the negative effects of competition shape and define nearly every aspect of modern life, including education, religion, politics, personal and international relations, sports, news, business and most of popular culture.

I have been on a long journey seeking answers to deeper questions about humanity's place in the world, and the fundamental problems confronting our species and our world. After years of searching piece by piece for the answers, the puzzle has finally come together for me. These fundamental societal problems arise and are passed on in the way we teach and learn. By introducing competition into every facet of our lives we undermine our ability to attain excellence, and perpetuate the problems we seek so desperately to resolve.

Evolutionary Education challenges the very foundation of our society. The first part of the book looks at the history of human culture in light of competition, and illuminates the "dark side" of our competitive system. It examines the real and alleged benefits of this system to show that it does not live up to its hype, and in fact causes more harm than good. (Even the relative few winners in our competitive system often pay a steep price, physically, mentally, emotionally, and spiritually, for their success.) It shows how the dominant competitive mindset into which we are all indoctrinated prevents us from questioning the validity of the competitive system, or recognizing or acknowledging its devastating effects on individuals and in society.

Evolutionary Education then offers an alternative, a non-competitive/cooperative educational model that I call Effortless Learning, which is described in detail in the course of the book. Competition takes its rightful place as an advanced aspect of an activity — an option, not a requirement. Something to be engaged in once competence in the fundamental skills can be demonstrated.

What I am proposing isn't theoretical, pie-in-the-sky conjecture. A viable, working program of Effortless Learning is in place. I have been teaching the highly competitive sport of tennis since 1974, helping many men, women, and children learn the game. Since October of 1992, however, this program has been based entirely on a non-competitive model of learning. In other words, there is no competition while people are learning the fundamentals of how to play the game.

My research in the seventeen years since I removed competition, which has included over ten thousand hours of on-court observation of close to a thousand different students, demonstrates that a non-competitive learning system can lead to tremendous success — even in competition. Effortless Learning sets us on the path to a more successful, cooperative, and joyful future.

The last part of the book shows how this non-competitive learning system can be applied in every area of our lives, and how it can help our species evolve to higher levels of consciousness. *Evolutionary Education* is a map and an invitation to join in a most important task – moving past our aggressive, competitive nature, whose dark side has led to inequality, poverty, injustice, abuse, war, and widespread mediocrity and malaise, toward a new era of cooperation, innovation, excellence, peace, and joy.

Reading this book will encourage you to search out your piece of the puzzle in the next stage of our human evolution. It will show you how to develop greater skill and excellence in your chosen field of endeavor. And that will make you happier, healthier, and more fulfilled, while making your world a better, more humane place to live, work, and play.

Brent Zeller
Summer 2007

Acknowledgments

Everlasting gratitude to my father and mother, John and Hazel Zeller. Without their love and support, I would never have had the time to assimilate all of the information contained in this book. My gratitude also goes to my brothers, Terry and Gary, who showed me that there is a big, diverse world out there.

Thanks to freelance editor Nancy Carleton of Berkeley, California, for getting the initial editing together, and to David Blake and Michael Katz for assisting her. Much appreciation to Doug Childers for taking the manuscript to a higher level and all the way home. Thanks to *Way of the Peaceful Warrior* author Dan Millman for providing inspiration over the years and for suggesting Nancy and Doug. Great thanks to Alfie Kohn for having the courage to challenge the competitive system. Thanks also to all of the people that read through the many incarnations of this manuscript and provided important feedback.

Extra special thanks to Robert Hunter, Jerry Garcia, and the Grateful Dead. As Robert penned and Jerry sang, "Sometimes you get shown the light in the strangest of places if you look at it right."

Brent Zeller
Summer 2007
Marin County, California

Introduction

Make no little plans.
Make the biggest plans you can think of,
and spend the rest of your life carrying them out.

— Harry S. Truman

It's been nearly 150 years since Charles Darwin wrote *On the Origin of Species*, and we are still seeking a key to unlock the secrets of the evolution of the human species. To fulfill our potential as a species, it is essential to come to a deeper understanding of the concept of evolution.

One definition of *evolution* is simply "change over time toward a more highly developed state." Things do change over time; no one can dispute that! Think of how children evolve in a few years from helpless little beings to people who can do things for themselves. Think of how electronics – cell phones, TV's, cameras and computers – have evolved within a short time frame. Such changes are examples of evolution. Evolution is a natural fact; it is nothing to be afraid of. Despite the recurrence of old controversies, accepting the reality of evolution doesn't rule out the existence of a Supreme Being. Belief or nonbelief in God can coexist with the concept of evolution. Whatever our religious beliefs, or lack thereof, it makes sense to understand how the human species has evolved until now — and how, and equally important, *where* it can evolve as we move forward.

PIECES OF THE PUZZLE

My interest in the evolution of our species arose as I grappled with several key events that took place while growing up in the 1960s.

The most important of these were the Civil Rights and women's movements; the assassinations of President Kennedy, Martin Luther King, Jr., and Bobby Kennedy; the blossoming and decline of the hippie movement; and the horrors of the Vietnam War. Watching these events unfold awakened in me a desire to help make the world a better, more peaceful place to live. I don't view this as a noble motive. I just didn't want to live in a world where violence and injustice were a norm that could potentially negatively impact my life. Of course good things were also happening, but the negatives made it hard for me to fully enjoy my life. I simply couldn't look the other way.

Since then, my life's goal has been to help make the world, and my own life, *significantly* better by working to transform destructive behaviors that have defined our species for thousands of years. Unfortunately, the world situation in regards to levels of violence and aggression is not that much different today. Some might say it's even worse. Technologically, we have advanced exponentially in the last two hundred years. But instinctively, our primal responses are not much different from those of our ancestors who roamed the savannas of Africa thousands of years ago.

Although at times I have been discouraged, somehow I've managed to keep my idealism alive and make it through my moments of doubt. We live on an incredible planet. We humans are amazing beings. Our accomplishments over the centuries are awe-inspiring. No one living a thousand years ago could have imagined *any* of what we take as commonplace today. As a species, our potential is virtually unlimited. But in order to achieve our potential, we need to ask and answer a few questions:

- With so many accomplishments to our credit, why is there still so much suffering in the world?

- With all of the extraordinary insights achieved from ancient spiritual traditions, philosophy and modern psychology, why does man's inhumanity prevail and produce so much stress, turmoil, despair, and sadness in so many people's lives?

- Are these realities unavoidable aspects of human nature? Is it simply our fate to possess virtually unlimited potential, yet forever limit that potential by behaving in ways that are petty, cruel, unconscious and self-destructive? Or do we have the ability to change?

I have spent nearly four decades pondering such questions, wondering what I can do – what all of us can do – to help move the evolution of our species forward, and move the world in a more positive direction. My longtime friends have called me a seeker. At some point, I started seeing life as a puzzle, and began looking to see how all the pieces might fit together into a harmonious whole.

Always searching for answers, I have read books, listened to speakers, and shared ideas with those who were willing to engage with me, or guide me. With each book, each speaker, and each intuition, another piece of that puzzle has fallen into place for me. As the pieces came together, it occurred to me that a core issue might underlie the negative aspects of human behavior, and a common thread might link the many manifestations of our suffering.

A Common Thread

The problems we face are diverse and complex. Some say they all stem from human laziness, greed, or evil: from inherently flawed human nature. But I have seen too many people display kindness, compassion, and courage to agree with that assessment.

As I examined the negative aspects of human behavior — over aggressiveness, anger, jealousy, fear, intimidation, violence, cheating, lying, and stealing — I kept noticing a common thread tying them together. That thread lies in competitive, aggressive behavior patterns, exacerbated by an innate survival instinct.

Currently, we live in a system predicated on a competitive model of behavior. We are raised to compete against one another from an early age. Unfortunately, this approach takes a serious toll on our psychological health and development, and thereby on our humanity. Competition is the norm for individuals, families, teams, tribes, communities, businesses, states, religions, and nations. In a way, life is one big contest, or a series of contests, marked by a constant jockeying for position in the pecking order. I'm better (smarter, stronger, faster, more beautiful, richer) than you are. My family is better than your family. Our community is better than your community. My school is better than your school. Our business, state, political party, country, or multi-national corporation is better than yours. My God is more powerful than your God. We are the chosen people and you are not!

We have been a competitive species for tens of thousands of years. And while that energy has motivated humanity to great accomplishments, it has also produced many of our darkest moments. Does having been a competitive species for so long mean we will be forever at war? Is this how it's supposed to be? This seems like a pretty bleak picture. I believe we have a choice; that we don't have to settle for this outcome.

In my search for answers, I have come to see competitive behavior as something we humans have learned over the course of our evolutionary history. Yes, in early times dangerous conditions forced humans to be more competitive to survive. But as societies developed, we transferred this competitive mentality into religion, commerce, relationships, politics, academics, and sports. Today, certain aspects of this mentality prevent us from fulfilling our greatest aspirations, and literally threaten our world.

LIMITATIONS OF A COMPETITIVE MINDSET

I do not advocate the elimination of competition. I do recommend that we examine where, when, and how competition creates problems, and seek healthy alternatives and solutions. Many people who call themselves highly competitive are simply people who have high expectations and a strong desire to succeed. The desire to be successful isn't, in and of itself, competitive. You can possess high expectations and a strong desire for success, yet not be competitive. We confuse the desire for excellence with the trait of competitiveness, when in truth they are very different.

A competitive mindset has led to great advances for our species, and provided a powerful motivating force for individuals, communities, nations and civilizations, but it is not the be-all and end-all of existence. From my youth, sports have been an integral part of my life. I have participated in, enjoyed (some of the time), and done well (a majority of the time) in thousands of contests. These competitive experiences have taught me many valuable lessons. Whether in sports, academics, business, or the arts, it is exciting and motivating to see people perform at a high level. I have no desire to take that away from anyone.

The problem is that only a small percentage of people succeed in this system, most function at a fraction of their potential. Is that because most people are not that bright or talented or motivated? Are they just mediocre, or lazy? In my experience, this is simply not the case. I have seen first hand how the competitive system itself inhibits development, and thus performance.

I am convinced that the problem is systemic and results in most of us functioning well below our potential. I believe our competitive system, by repeatedly pitting us against each other in often premature and needlessly adversarial contests, destabilizes our confidence and motivation, and limits our ability, our enjoyment, and our overall development. I will show the evidence for these assertions in the following chapters.

TIME FOR A COURSE CORRECTION

Over the centuries, the competitive mindset has become the dominant model of behavior for a majority of people. I believe it is time to make some healthy changes in this model, which I will discuss later. I am basically an optimist. But as a longtime student of history and current events, I am aware that if we don't change course soon, life may get ugly, not for just a few, but for most. The crux of the problem inherent in a competitive paradigm is that *each generation must be more competitive than the last, not to achieve an absolute standard of excellence, but just to keep up.* **Each generation must be more competitive!** The big question is, how much more competitive can we be? When does the stress of this unrealistic expectation begin producing more negative than positive results? And have we already reached that point?

Many people are uncertain and anxious about their future, and are doing all they can to keep up. Millions don't get enough to eat on a daily basis. Greed and fear are present at every level from politics to business, to social institutions. Destruction and contamination of vital ecosystems is a planet-wide problem. Ethnic violence and prejudice are rampant around the globe. Our weapons of mass destruction make it possible for us to obliterate ourselves at any moment. I could provide many more such examples of the competitive mindset being out of control, but I am sure you get the point. This is no way to live — *for anyone*. And yet, it's the way *almost everyone lives.*

We need to make major changes. I'm not talking about *revolution*, but *higher evolution*. Revolution entails an "us versus them" dynamic – a competitive mindset. In a revolution, one group works to overthrow those in power and take charge themselves. Most revolutions are rooted in anger and turn ugly and violent. Revolutions are examples of how the Darwinian law of the jungle has fueled our evolutionary process as a species. But eventually, our higher evolution will allow us to see that everyone is on the same side, working toward the same goal, and that making life better for everyone makes it better for ourselves.

Again, this book does not propose to banish competition. Rather, it examines the dynamics of competition and the many societal and inter-personal problems it causes. It looks to see if competition in fact produces the best attainable results; to see where and when competition is appropriate and effective, and where it isn't.

Modern advances in technology have made Earth a very small planet. Whether we like it or not, we are all in this together. And we can all be part of the solutions to our collective problems. As Charles Darwin noted, "The survival or extinction of each organism is determined by that organism's ability to adapt to its environment." The same is true for a species. This book is a call for a new adaptation of human behavior in our increasingly changing and challenging environment. Our survival may depend upon it!

PART ONE
Current Reality

Picture a bright blue ball just spinning, spinning free
Dizzy with eternity

A peaceful place or so it looks from space
A closer look reveals the human race
Full of hope, full of grace, the human face
But afraid we may lay our home to waste

If the game is lost then we're all the same
No one left to place or take the blame
Will we leave this place an empty stone
Or that shining ball of blue we call our home

There's a whole world full of petty wars
I got mine and you got yours
And the current fashion sets the pace
Lose your step fall out of grace
Well, the radical he rants in rage
Singing someone's got to turn the page

The rich man in his summer home
Saying, just leave well enough alone
But his pants are down, his cover's blown
And the politicians are throwing stones
It's all too clear we are on our own

Picture a bright blue ball just spinning, spinning free
Dizzy with possibilities

— John Barlow

1
Human Nature and the Evolutionary Process

The basic question about human nature
isn't whether humans are basically peaceful or basically violent —
for we are both —
but which of the two are we going to organize.

— Joan Baez

IN THE BEGINNING

Figuring out how far back competition goes is easy; it's in our history books, and our most ancient scriptures and stories, passed on orally from generation to generation before the written word. The theme of most significant events from our earliest recorded history is conquest. The stories, written by the victors, are about chiefs, kings, emperors and generals vanquishing their adversaries. Their legacy is competition and domination. War, the ultimate competition, has become a model for most of our enterprises.

Obviously, the competitive mentality goes back much further than recorded history. Anthropologists and archeologists trace this tribal mentality back to our primordial past. Has it always been this way, or was there ever a more cooperative time? Over the last thirty years a significant body of evidence has emerged from the archeological record suggesting that prior to about five thousand years ago a more cooperative culture flourished in the Near East, the Middle East, and on into Central Europe. The archeological record since then points to societies based on a hierarchical, competitive model. But before that, at least for a portion of the planet, evidence indicates that a different model prevailed.

At the religious and burial sites of these older societies dating back to Paleolithic and Neolithic times, archeologists have found a preponderance of female figurines. These artifacts from the Paleolithic period date back thirty thousand years, and those from the Neolithic date back about ten thousand years. Archeologists surmise that these figurines relate to worship of the feminine — evidence of a goddess culture. In later cultures, male deity figures are common in burial sites.

Examples of Neolithic paintings and other art depicting scenes of religious ceremonies centering around a female figure also abound. Feminine figurines and symbols occupied a central place in the mythology of this time. And in the art of the Neolithic era discovered so far, scenes of battles, conquering heroes, and even weapons are conspicuously absent. Excavations of many sites from this period do not reveal a hierarchical pattern of a few grand structures and many small ones, but a more egalitarian pattern, with most buildings similar in size. Nor did these sites reveal structures with a high level of fortification common to war-like cultures. Archeologists postulate that these societies were more egalitarian, with everyone closer to equal in status, and less war-like than later cultures. Excavations of later sites reveal much greater variability in building size, indicating a more hierarchical social system, with an abundance of fortification.

The historian Riane Eisler, in her highly acclaimed book *The Chalice and the Blade*, documents evidence of a culture that included a more egalitarian approach to living, which she calls a *partnership model*. Archeological research indicates that between five thousand and seven thousand years ago, groups of invaders, which Eisler calls *dominator races* (and which history books have called the Mongol hordes), came into these areas from the north and east. Through conquest these invaders displaced the cooperative cultures with their hierarchical ones. The archeological record provides a large body of evidence that these dominator cultures placed their religious sites directly on top of the earlier sites, attempting to erase any evidence of what came before.

The likelihood of a more cooperatively based culture somewhere in our past is important to our understanding of the history of competition. It lets us know that the current competitive model is not the only option. Another approach has at least been tried, and appears to have prospered for a time.

In any case, over the last five thousand years encompassing written history, the record is clear: Competition has been king. Hierarchical societies have been the norm. Domination, not cooperation, has been the rule. For the most part, those of us living today are descended from the winners of this dominator mentality. Our ancestors were those who survived the battles. We inherited their characteristics. No wonder many of us are competitive and aggressive.

SURVIVAL OF THE FITTEST?

Because this competitive model has dominated for so long, many people believe that we are aggressive and competitive by nature and nothing can be done to change this behavior. The idea that human nature is inherently competitive received validation in the mid-1800s from the work of Charles Darwin. With his theory of evolution, Darwin presented a vast body of evidence that all life on Earth evolved over millions of years from a few common ancestors. This evolution occurred through a process called *natural selection.*

From his research and observations, Darwin noted that possessing certain traits increased a species chance of survival; a higher percentage of animals with these traits would survive and, through procreation, pass them on genetically to the next generation. For example, when the climate grew significantly colder, animals with thicker fur would survive in disproportionate numbers. In a drought, animals that could survive on less water would endure.

Darwin's theory promoted the idea of the *survival of the fittest.* This term is a bit misleading since the individuals possessing traits that increased their chances of survival had nothing to do with developing those traits. The male bird with brighter colors that made him more attractive to females did not control the amount of color in his feathers. The individual members of a species that survived dramatic climate change did not intentionally change their makeup in order to survive. It wasn't survival of the fittest so much as the good fortune of those whose traits happened to suit the demands of the time.

Inevitably, supporters of a competitive worldview commandeered Darwin's concept in order to prove that being competitive was natural and superior to all other ways of interacting. This view became known as Social Darwinism. When two animals fight to the death it is easy to conclude that the winner is the stronger, more competitive animal. The twisted logic of Social Darwinism holds that aggressive, competitive individuals are the most suited, and therefore the most deserving, of survival and success in life. Thus competition is viewed as natural and even essential to our progress and development.

Dog-eat-dog competition, seen as human nature, now defines most aspects of business, politics, sports, and even popular culture. It's the new mode of popular entertainment, from TV's Survivor, American Idol and The Apprentice, to the slew of programs that reduce "contestants" to the level of aggressive beasts hunting and fighting for survival around the drought-ravaged watering hole. There's no disputing the potential in almost all species for highly competitive and aggressive behavior. And we human beings are an animal species. But does this prove the inevitability or the superiority, of competitive behavior? On the surface, this can seem to be the case. But if we look more closely, we see that competitive behavior manifests most frequently and intensely when there is a shortage of some necessity, like water, food, shelter, sex or, with the animal called Man, money.

Competitive behavior manifests when we are threatened or our survival is at stake, and even when there is an illusory perception of a threat. Nature reveals that when there is no shortage in the necessities of survival, there is less competitive, aggressive behavior. And both animals and man thrive best when they cooperate with one another. This is why most animals form herds, packs and flocks, and why man formed tribes, villages, towns and nations.

SURVIVAL OF THE LUCKIEST

Sometimes survival of the fittest becomes survival of the luckiest, or even weakest. This was the case for one troop of savanna baboons in Kenya studied by researchers Robert Sapolsky and Lisa Share starting in 1978. Baboons, like chimpanzees and humans, are known to be quite hierarchical and male-dominated, with frequent aggressive interactions. Between 1983 and 1986, the troop's dominant males, who were observed to be very aggressive, were wiped out by contracting bovine tuberculosis through foraging in the garbage dump at a nearby tourist lodge. The lesser males and the females did not contract the disease because the dominant males prevented them from feeding at the dump. The deaths of the dominant males drastically changed the gender composition of the troop, more than doubling the ratio of females to males, and by 1986 troop behavior had changed dramatically; males were now significantly less aggressive.

Observation of the troop stopped after 1986 and did not start again until 1993. At this time, the same less-aggressive behavior was observed in the troop. This is particularly surprising and enlightening because male baboons leave their birth troop after puberty. Even though there were few adult males from the previous period, the new males showed the less-aggressive behavior of their predecessors. Apparently, the adolescent baboons observing the interactions between the females and the older males of the troop learned that they didn't have to be as aggressive to get what they needed! The researchers even analyzed blood samples from the troop during this second period of observation and found that the males lacked the distinctive physiological markers of stress normally found in male baboons in other areas.

Another anomaly is the *bonobos*, a Central African species of Great Ape closely related to chimpanzees and humans. Bonobo behavior is quite different than the average ape or human. Interactions in bonobo society are more egalitarian and peaceful – they typically resolve their differences by grooming one another or having some type of sexual contact. Sounds more civilized to me!

Evolutionary biologist, Dr. Lynn Margulis, has demonstrated that symbiotic relationships are a major driving force in evolution. A symbiotic relationship is one in which two or more dissimilar organisms live together, especially when this association is mutually beneficial. In other words, cooperation is fundamental to the nature of life and the evolutionary process. Margulis and her world-renowned husband, scientist Carl Sagan, concluded in 1996 "Life did not take over the globe by combat, but by networking" (i.e. by cooperation, interaction, and mutual dependence between living organisms).

NON-COMPETITIVE INDIVIDUALS AND COOPERATION

The instinct to survive *is* part of our human nature, but a survival instinct is different from a competitive instinct. A survival instinct usually becomes competitive when there is a perceived scarcity and others are trying to get what we need. For competitive behavior to truly be an immutable aspect of human nature, *everyone* would have to be competitive, and this is simply not the case. We all know people in our lives that are not the least bit competitive. Prime examples of people with a cooperative worldview would include Jesus, Mahatma Gandhi, Martin Luther King, Jr., Rumi, Mother Theresa, many spiritual practitioners of many faiths, quite a few members of the helping professions, and members of several indigenous tribes that still survive around the world. As psychologist Alfie Kohn has noted, "The ubiquity of cooperative interactions even in a relatively competitive society is powerful evidence against the generalization that humans are naturally competitive." Cooperation is every bit as natural as competition.

LEARNED BEHAVIOR

Although competitive behavior has been with us for thousands of years, much of this behavior has been consciously programmed into us from childhood on by our parents, schools, athletics programs, governments, even our churches, and many other respected institutions. To paraphrase Alfie Kohn, competition has been a part of the subtext of almost every lesson we have learned. No wonder it seems natural. Having something reinforced and promoted over thousands of years deeply ingrains it in our nature. But the examples in this chapter support the view that some of this programming is learned; and suggest that it is possible to unlearn it, and evolve to a less destructive and more productive way of being.

In 1937, in one of the largest studies on competition in its time, psychologists Mark A. May and Leonard Doob concluded: "Human beings by original nature strive for goals, but striving with others or against others are learned forms of behavior. Neither of these two can be said to be the more genetically basic, fundamental or primordial." To this we can add the thoughts of sports psychologists Thomas Tutko and William Bruns: "People are not *born* with a motivation to win or to be competitive. We inherit a potential for a degree of activity, and we all have the instinct to survive. But the will to win comes through training and the influences of one's family and environment."

Clearly, competitive behavior has been programmed into us, and become part of our human nature. Now let's consider the possibility that we can alter this deep programming.

HUMAN GENETICS RESEARCH

Cellular biologist Dr. Bruce Lipton, in his research on human genetics, provides evidence that our genes do not ultimately control our behavior. This evidence goes against one of the popular beliefs about biology, that our genes determine our traits and behaviors, which are therefore largely predetermined. For over fifty years, many scientists, with the assistance of the media, have presented as scientific fact this idea of our fates being written in our genetic code.

As a result, many people do believe that we are genetically preprogrammed, and therefore have little control over our behavior. This view is the scientific Nature side of the classic Nature versus Nurture debate. The Nurture side believes that human behavior is mostly determined by conditioning. The truth likely includes a mixture of both.

Cutting-edge cellular biologists like Dr. Lipton now recognize that our environment and, more importantly, our perceptions of our environment strongly affect the activity of our genes. We have tendencies toward certain behavior, but these tendencies aren't immutable. Even if the *potential* for aggressive, competitive behavior is encoded in our DNA, it isn't necessarily our destiny.

This new research indicates that, rather than being at the mercy of our genes, our behavior is also influenced by what we perceive to be our environment. Our genes are turned on and off by our perceptions and beliefs, whether these perceptions and beliefs are true or false. As we saw earlier with regard to scarcity, what we perceive as real doesn't have to be real to affect our behavior. Experiencing fear doesn't mean danger is present; yet we feel and may even act *as if* we are in danger. Believing something is true doesn't make it objectively true, yet it does seem to make it appear real *subjectively*. This new research suggests that cells respond to our perceptions by triggering either growth, or protective behaviors. If our perceptions are accurate, the resulting behavior is generally beneficial to us. But if we are operating from misperceptions, our behavior will likely be inappropriate and lead to undesirable results.

Learned perceptions, especially those derived from parents, peers, academic education, advertising, religion, or propaganda, may be based upon incorrect information or faulty interpretations. We often run into problems with religious, political, or philosophical beliefs, since people may act on these beliefs as if they were fundamental truths despite valid and even overwhelming evidence to the contrary. People tend to become dogmatic around their beliefs. The good news is that perceptions and beliefs can be relearned. We can alter our behaviors by retraining our consciousness.

This understanding of what influences our behavior has deepened with the completion of the Human Genome Project. In 1990, the Human Genome Project undertook an ambitious goal, to map the entire human genetic code, a project finished in 2003. Before scientists completed mapping the genetic code, there was general agreement that an organism as complex as a human would have approximately one hundred thousand genes. By comparison, a microscopic organism such as a roundworm has eighteen thousand genes. To their surprise, and probable dismay, the geneticists of the Human Genome Project found that humans had only about twenty-five thousand genes, far too few to control our biology and behavior. Genetically, we are not much more complex than a microscopic roundworm! Talk about humbling. Because of the relatively small number of genes found, we can't attribute our individual character to genetic programming.

CELLULAR MEMORY

Something we can attribute our programming to is *cellular memory*. The mechanism of cellular memory patterns actions and behaviors into our subconscious, without our conscious help. This process is always happening. It is our natural learning system, and without it we wouldn't be able to survive. Whatever we repeat, we remember on a deep level — whether these actions are physical, mental, or emotional. We see this on its simplest level when a young child mimics the behavior of others. After just a short time of mimicking, the child exhibits this behavior automatically, without thinking. This is why the multiplication tables are taught through repetition; eventually, children remember the answer without having to think about it. This is how long-term learning works. Cellular memory is what allows long-term learning. It is also what often keeps us trapped in habitual, non-productive behaviors. And, it can also enable us to tap into the positive forces of evolution and overcome old, negative, conditioned patterns of thinking and behavior.

Cellular memory is distributed throughout the body; much cellular learning happens in the brain, but much happens in the rest of the body as well. Nerve impulse travels between ten and three hundred feet per second, depending on the diameter of the nerve cells along the pathway. If reflex memory were stored entirely in the brain, its signals wouldn't be able to reach the limbs quickly enough. A lot of reflex memory is stored in the spine. Otherwise, none of us would be able to appreciate the beauty of an arpeggio on the piano or the artistry of Roger Federer on the tennis court — the communication between the player's head and hands would take too long. All of the cells involved in a muscular response are permanently affected by repetitive learning, and contribute to the response. This is also true with mental and emotional responses.

Recent research in neurobiology shows that a substance called myelin coats neurons as a kind of insulating agent. This insulation thickens as an action is repeated. Neurobiologists believe that this insulating process works to keep a strong signal between neurons by preventing electrical impulses from leaking out. The thicker the myelin, the faster and more accurately the signals travel. This is the physiological process that results in cellular memory.

The problem is that over the years we have programmed many negative behaviors – or as I prefer to call them, less-than-optimal responses— into our cellular memory. And when certain actions or behaviors are ingrained in our cellular memory, it becomes more difficult, though not impossible, to change them.

On one level, we are amazingly complex beings who can speak a multitude of languages and create mind defying inventions and masterpieces of art. On another level, we are incredibly simple beings, much like Pavlov's dogs, whose repetitive behaviors etch patterns into our cells, for good and ill. It happens automatically.

We have all heard that we are creatures of habit; this is our cellular memory at work. With a computer, we type something in to the hard drive once, and it's there whenever we wish to access it. For humans, it takes a certain amount of repetition until something is patterned. With cellular memory, however, there is no delete button. Once something is in the cells, it is there for life, unless we pattern something else in, which unfortunately takes an even more concerted, yet identical effort.

DEEPLY PROGRAMMED BEHAVIOR

Competitive behavior has been deeply wired into most people's cellular memory. The fact that many people find it difficult to imagine an alternative to competitive behavior shows how deeply programmed this belief has become. Psychologist Alfie Kohn has observed: "That most of us fail to consider the alternatives to competition is a testament to the effectiveness of our socialization. We have been trained not only to compete but to believe in competition." Along these lines, sociologist David Riesman has stated, "First we are systematically socialized to compete — and to want to compete — and then the results are cited as evidence of competition's inevitability."

A great example of this socialization is in youth sports. Before children's minds have developed to the point where they can think independently for themselves, they are put into competition against one another. Of course they are going to believe that being competitive with each other is the way life is — because the authority figures in their lives are telling them that this is how it is, and so it seems natural.

This competitive belief is so much a part of our being that it is like air to us. It is all around us, so familiar that we often can't see it, so ingrained that we instinctively reach for it, imagining that our survival depends upon it. Few people question the rightness, effectiveness or inevitability of competition. Like oxygen, we can't imagine living without it; unlike oxygen, we can actually thrive without it.

Another factor accounts for people's reluctance to shift from an unhealthy competitive model to a healthy but unfamiliar non-competitive model. Most of us naturally resist change, are reluctant to take risks, and wish to avoid uncertainty. We tend to stick with what is familiar even if it isn't working well for us. This is why people stay in abusive relationships, unpleasant and unsatisfying jobs, and continue to repeat ineffective behaviors.

Yet healthy change almost always involves some discomfort and resistance. For a variety of reasons, old patterns die hard. I will show in the following chapters that, despite any difficulties that may arise in the process of changing from a competitive to a non-competitive system, the benefits of making the shift will be extraordinary and culturally transforming. Millions of people over many generations have been "defeated" and turned off to learning by our competitive educational system. It is time to undo that harm by changing the system that inflicts it.

I will also show how the Effortless Learning program has proven that we can learn and excel in a non-competitive environment; undo old limiting physical and psychological habits and patterns and replace them with new positive ones; have more fun in the learning process; and even go on to succeed in a competitive environment if we so desire. A non-competitive learning model will help adults transcend the damage done by years of immersion in an unhealthy competitive system. It will keep children from ever being subjected to this damage, and in the process will produce great champions, and a healthier human race.

In the end, whether competition is part of human nature or not isn't as important as the fact that we have the ability to alter our programming and fulfill our greater potential as individuals and as a species. This book suggests that a different kind of learning can replace an old, outdated, limited program with a new more healthy and effective program for learning and for living. Before we examine the benefits of non-competitive learning and the solutions this approach offers, it is necessary to fully illuminate the issues and problems with the current competitive system.

Almost ablaze still you don't feel the heat.
Takes all you got just to stay on the beat.
You say it's a living we've all got to eat.
But you're here alone, there's no one to compete.
If Mercy's in business, I wish it for you,
More than just ashes when your dreams come true.
Fire, Fire on the Mountain.

—Robert Hunter

2

A Competitive Learning System

For many children competitive sports operate as a failure factory which not only effectively eliminates the "bad ones" but also turns off many of the good ones.

— Terry Orlick

Our social framework is based on competition, so it follows that our educational system is also competitively based. Hardly anyone can imagine sports, education, business, or politics without competition. From a young age, we find that virtually every activity in which we participate includes some form of competition. Whether in school or sports, shortly after we get involved, we face an opponent in one form or another. When we're graded on a curve, when we take the PSAT to prepare us for the SAT, and even when we are asked to raise our hands if we know the answer, we are competing against other students.

Few of us question the competitive approach. We tend to think of it as organic and essential; people must compete to succeed, the logic goes, so they had better get used to the pressures of competition from the start. The problem is not with competition per se, but how and when we go about having people compete.

PREMATURE COMPETITION

Introducing competition into the learning process prematurely — before we master fundamental skills — causes many problems. This is perhaps most obvious in the field of sports, so I will use that arena to illustrate this concept. It is not uncommon to see five-year-olds playing competitive soccer games after two weeks of practice, which as a rule means two one-hour practices. What skill level can be achieved in two hours? Many teams practice very little together once they start playing their weekly game; often their weekly competition is their *only* practice. This is putting the cart before the horse! These children need to spend non-competitive time running around the field, having fun, kicking the ball to one another, getting fit and coordinated, practicing and developing their skills, and allowing cellular memory to pattern the basics into their body/minds *before* competition enters the picture.

This competitive approach is common in youth sports. In baseball I've seen seven-years-old pitchers who couldn't throw the ball over the plate, and batters who couldn't make contact with a slowly pitched ball. Why do we make these kids compete before they've learned the basic skills? One of the few sports where competition is postponed until fundamental skills have been developed is gymnastics. This is because gymnastics can be very dangerous, and the consequences of premature competition (before developing fundamental skills) are potentially severe.

Even when children aren't competing against one another on a conscious level, they are often being pushed to get to the point where they can compete. This so called *games-based* approach to learning is widespread. Players are supposed to learn their skills *while* playing competitively. Indeed, some learning is going on during competition, but a lot of it negatively impacts a player's development. Many skills are not being developed, and many less than optimal habits are being patterned into the physical, mental, and emotional cellular memory.

In the competitive system, winners are lionized; the rest are second-class citizens, often regarded as also-rans, or worse, losers. The world of competition is a jungle. Is it really a good idea to expose children to this jungle before they are prepared physically, mentally, and emotionally? It is hard enough even when they *are* prepared. The question to ask is whether the competitive system truly produces excellence, or just a set of winners of uncertain ability? With winning such a premium and so strongly desired, it would make sense at the very least to learn the essential skills of an activity before being thrust into competition. But that is not how we are taught.

Many assume that exposing children to competition at an early age prepares them for all the competition they will face throughout life. But as you will see, this is not the case. This is the drop-the-baby-in-the-deep-end-of-the-pool theory of learning. If the "baby" sinks instead of swimming, it is assumed, in the competitive mind-set, not to "have what it takes." Putting people, especially children, into competition before they have developed effective skills, can be painful, even traumatic. Many will be scarred emotionally. The resulting embarrassment, shame or lowered self-esteem will hold them back in other areas of life, and diminish their chances of achieving their potential.

When a society places so much importance on winning, losing is often experienced as personal failure. We've all heard that it doesn't matter if we win or lose, it's how we play the game. But these hollow words do not reflect the reality we see all around us, and the message we are "told" in countless ways. The winner gets it all — the praise, the glory, the fame, and the fortune. Even young children can see and feel that it *does* matter whether we win or lose; and that there are real benefits to winning, and real consequences to losing.

WINNING VERSUS LEARNING

The competitive approach to learning is widespread in all aspects of education. Children find themselves in a recital or a performance after taking only a few months of music or dance lessons. If children *really* know and can proficiently play or perform the material, no problem. If not, they are programming performance anxiety into their cellular memory. I know this from personal experience. From starting piano lessons at age six, to playing drums in the band in high school, I was put into performances before I was confident of the material. Those experiences sowed the seeds of a lack of confidence, and performance anxiety.

Academically, it's the same: Children are given material to learn, and then tested and graded before they have *really* learned that material. What are we really testing and teaching by putting children into competition prematurely? And what are children really learning in this way?

This is the trial by fire or school-of-hard-knocks approach to learning: "We learned the hard way; you have to learn the hard way. Life isn't fair, life is tough!" Maybe life is tough. Do we need to make it tougher on principle? Maybe we did learn the hard way. Do we have to make learning harder for everyone? How about discovering what may actually be the best way to learn? The school-of-hard-knocks approach does push a small percentage of people to excel, primarily from fear of the consequences of failure, or perhaps an overweening desire to win or to be number one. But *most people fail to achieve their potential in a competitive environment.* Even those who succeed often pay a steep price, physically, mentally, and emotionally. Yet this is the environment in which we continue to raise and educate our children. What are we passing on?

When learning becomes a contest, the focus shifts from learning skills to winning contests, and to fears of losing. When being a winner is so important, it can't help taking precedence over developing the skills necessary to achieve excellence. And this is a fundamental problem in our competitive culture.

POSITIVE EFFECTS OF A COMPETITIVE SYSTEM

There is no disputing the fact that competition has produced many tangible benefits in people's lives. It encourages us to work toward goals and develop concentration, perseverance, motivation and ambition. It can help us hone our skills, raise performance levels, strive for excellence, build character, and even foster camaraderie and teamwork while channeling aggression in a less destructive direction.

We have seen the benefits of a competitive approach in industry where competing companies, teams and individuals stimulate higher levels of creativity and leap-frog off each other, inventing or designing better and better products and technologies. Such competition has fostered rapid growth and accelerated technological breakthroughs in many fields. A clear example of competition motivating accelerated development is the space race between the United States and the U.S.S.R. back in the 1960's that resulted in the U.S. sending the first man to the moon.

Yet despite all the benefits of a competitive paradigm, I suggest that our next stage of evolution will enable us to achieve far more benefits through non-competition, which includes a skill-to-mastery based focus, and a higher principle of cooperation.

This chapter focuses mainly on the negative side effects of competition. (The benefits of competition have been actively promoted for centuries, if not millennia. We all know them quite well.) It will show why the premature introduction of competition into the learning process produces far more negative than positive effects. In fact, *if competition were a drug, the Food and Drug Administration would ban it for having too many adverse side effects!*

Let's look at some of these adverse effects.

DRAWBACKS OF THE COMPETITIVE SYSTEM

First, to understand how easily human behavior can be negatively influenced by an underlying system, consider a famous psychology experiment conducted at Stanford University in 1971 by Professor Phillip Zimbardo. In this experiment Zimbardo set up a prison environment in a basement of one of the university buildings, then randomly divided his students into roles of prisoner or guard.

The experiment, designed to last for two weeks, was terminated before the end of the first week due to the severity of the results, which included radical behavioral changes in virtually all of the participants. Within several days the student/guards began abusing the "prisoners", who rapidly succumbed to a victim mentality. This experiment clearly demonstrated how profoundly a system can affect the behavior of the people within it, even to the point of distorting their usual personalities, behaviors and previously held values. In the following section, I show how the competitive system produces specific negative behavioral effects in ordinary people.

Dampens Motivation

Initially, competition does produce motivation as we strive to be winners, but mounting losses can quickly undermine that motivation. If losing continues, staying motivated can be a Herculean task. Many sports psychologists are now saying that to maintain competitive motivation, participants need to win two out of every three contests they enter. Because most people don't win anywhere close to that percentage, motivation frequently wanes; after a certain percentage of "failure", resignation often occurs. This is why so many people drift from one activity to another, looking for a place where they can be successful — where they can be winners.

There's another disturbing aspect to a competitive approach.

Researchers have found that we only stay motivated if the rewards increase. After a period of time, if the rewards don't increase, motivation levels tend to decrease. This is a common phenomenon in professional sports. How often have we heard of athletes who are already making millions of dollars wanting to renegotiate their contract because they feel they are worth more? If they don't get their way, their motivation drops.

Lowers Performance Levels

Contrary to popular belief, competition actually lowers performance levels for almost all participants. Yes, competition can induce motivation in many instances. But as I have noted, much of this motivation involves fear of the consequences of failure. Psychologist Alfie Kohn, who has long explored the dynamics of competition, noted, "We are carefully trained to believe that a competitive arrangement results in superior performance." From his research, Kohn concluded: "Superior performance not only does not *require* competition; it usually seems to require its absence." The pressure of needing to win makes people tighten up, which universally lowers performance levels.

In a study completed in 1981, researchers David and Roger Johnson and colleagues published a paper analyzing the results of 122 different studies that examined whether competitive or cooperative environments induced higher performance. The results were eye opening: Over half the studies indicated that cooperation produced higher performance levels, more than one-third showed no statistical advantage to either cooperation or competition, and less than 10 percent showed a competitive environment producing higher performance. Philosopher John McMurtry concluded: "The pursuit of victory works to reduce the chance for excellence in the true performance of the sport. It tends to distract our attention from excellence of performance by rendering it subservient to emerging victorious."

Diminishes Enjoyment

Competition is most enjoyable for winners. For "losers" it is rarely exciting or enjoyable. This is especially true when we consistently lose more than we win, which is the case for the majority. *I have never met anyone who didn't like winning, nor met anyone who enjoys losing!* We see this in fans living and dying with their team; ecstatic when their team is winning, and angry or depressed when they are losing.

The "thrill of victory" adrenaline rush can become an addiction. Many people compete in one way or another for their whole lives, seeking the high that winning gives them. It makes them feel good about themselves; makes them feel they matter and are worthy. Many people use competition as a means to get approval and self-esteem. But the downside to chronic competition is that when winning is over-emphasized, our perspective becomes skewed and our character often becomes unbalanced. We lose sight of other more important values, like cooperation, trust, compassion, and the development of true human maturity.

Raises Stress Levels

People today are under a great deal of stress, whether from work, school, family, sports, relationships, or from having to adapt to a rapidly changing world. Since 9/11, stress levels have increased in a large segment of the American population, across all socioeconomic groups. The negative effects of stress include increased physical and emotional tension, uncertainty and fear, a weakening of the immune system, decline in health, and less overall enjoyment of life. Must we add to the unavoidable stresses of life the unnecessary burden of ubiquitous competition?

There is pressure and tension all around us, and we accept it as natural or at least inevitable. But are we like the proverbial frog that, when put into water that is slowly heated to a boil, calmly lets itself be cooked to death?

Undermines Healthy Character Development

One of the main benefits attributed to competition by supporters is that it develops character. But it can be equally shown that competition undermines, weakens and retards the development of real character, or human maturity. In a competitive environment we are taught to view others as adversaries, to find their weaknesses and exploit them, and even to use psychological tactics and strategies to distract and destabilize them. A competitive system often breeds hostile, mistrustful relationships between opponents, and a hostile environment. *Competition can even turn friends into adversaries.*

The "best" competitors show no compassion to their opponents; compassion could mean the difference between winning and losing! We must destroy their confidence, or they might defeat us! This approach pays dividends in the present, and in future encounters with our defeated opponents, over whom we establish a psychological advantage. In my forty-five years of experience in sports, I've seen this strategy taught, with no malice of intent, by a majority of successful coaches. These coaches believe that it is essential to instill this "competitive attitude" or "killer instinct" in people who are going to be winners at a high level.

A competitive mindset keeps many from developing admirable character traits, not to mention fulfilling their highest potential. Given the misbehavior we often see in competitions of various kinds, it might even be argued that the competitive mindset is a form of temporary insanity. It is much easier to maintain high ideals and play by the rules when we are winning. Once we start losing, however, the possibility that we will resort to negative alternatives to increase our chances of winning — such as overly aggressive behavior, intimidation, and cheating —increases. You have to win to be seen as a winner, and a certain percentage of people will do whatever it takes to make that happen. Highly competitive environments encourage a win-at-all-cost mentality that is a major contributor to destabilizing character development.

Conversely, those who don't do well in competitive environments may end up avoiding all competition, which can also weaken character. Chronic failure undermines self-confidence, lowers self-esteem, produces feelings of inferiority, stimulates frustration, anger, resignation, sadness, and even depression and despair. Being told it is okay to lose doesn't change this; we all know "losers" are looked down on in our competitive culture.

In a competitive system, the only way feelings of inferiority can be avoided is by winning enough to balance out the losses. This is problematic. Because by design the competitive system creates far more losers than winners, *most* people never win enough to balance out their losses. Feelings of inferiority stay with them, often for a lifetime. Feeling inferior may provide motivation to improve and excel, but in the long run it doesn't bring out the best in us, nor help us to be our best.

I have seen the results of this cycle manifested with tennis players and other athletes. People who have lost a lot need to balance out their feelings of inferiority in order to feel good about themselves. A corrosive striving for superiority over others often arises from these experiences. Some go from one competitive activity to another, looking for a place where they can be the winners. The truth is that, in a competitive system, losers need to defeat somebody and exact their revenge in order to feel better about themselves. It takes a long time and a lot of positive feedback to change this dynamic. In a competitive environment, it's extremely difficult to make up the deficit.

Finally, the more success we achieve in a competitive environment, the more people want to beat us. Like Old West gunfighters, we have to be constantly on the alert, looking over our shoulder to make sure no one is gunning for us. It's easy to get a little edgy and make poor decisions in this environment. Emotions such as fear and anger can motivate us, but they don't serve us well as dominant character traits. Yet these emotions tend to be forged in competitive environments, and through premature competition.

Ingrains Inadequate Basic Skills

When we are put into competition too soon, we try everything we can to win, because that's the goal. But we often forget our basic skills and unconsciously resort to ineffective reactions. This is very apparent in people who start playing competitive tennis before they've developed their fundamental physical skills. Almost immediately, the correct form they've been practicing degenerates until they look more like they are fending off an attacker than playing tennis. It's not a pretty sight.

Unfortunately, whatever we *are* doing (and what we are feeling) is being programmed into our cellular memory, to become ingrained habit. Inadequate preparation of basic skills, combined with competition, limits our skill development, and increases the development of bad habits. We may do relatively well initially with inadequate skills, but eventually it works against us.

Ideally we will go back and develop the pieces that we missed. But this doesn't always happen. Learning a second language provides an apt example here. If we are rushing through the learning process, it is easy to pattern grammatically incorrect sentence structure or inappropriate use of a word into our cellular memory. Someone may be able to understand our meaning, but our statements lose some of their power. Undoing a negative pattern takes far more effort than learning correctly from the start. Inadequate preparation of basic skills is a big problem in most people's development across all disciplines. Once again, trying to win trumps learning the skills.

Cultivates Winning Without Skill

In every contest there is a winner. In a few cases there is a draw. But being declared a winner doesn't mean you have developed proper skills or achieved competence, let alone mastery. Participants competing prematurely in any sport or endeavor exhibit more luck than ability, and certainly very little skill. In fact, most contests are lost, not won; they are decided by the loser making too many errors. Yet someone still gets the reward of being called the winner.

Even at the professional level, contests are commonly marred by less-than-optimal play and behavior. (In Chapter 5, I'll explain why I prefer the term *less-than-optimal* instead of *bad*). All too often, even professional athletes play well below their abilities — a baseball or football player dropping an easy catch, a basketball player missing an open shot, a tennis player missing an easy volley, or a soccer or hockey player not scoring a goal on a one-on-one break. At the 2004 French Open Women's Championships Venus Williams lost a match by making eighty-seven (!) unforced errors out of a total of one hundred points that she lost. Venus is a great tennis player, but her performance that day was pure mediocrity. Her opponent won only thirteen points in the entire match on her own. Yet she "won" the match.

Why do professional athletes tighten up, lose concentration, and miss easy shots that, at their level, they should not miss? In most sports there are situations where events are almost completely within our control. In tennis, it is the serve; we have the ball in our hands. In basketball it is the free throw; no one is blocking our shot. And professionals have been practicing these shots for years, probably tens of thousands of times. Yet even professionals frequently miss in these unchallenged moments. Clearly the problem is between their ears, and ingrained in their cellular memories. To me such incidents illustrate that even top athletes have been limited by premature competition. Their basic psychological skills are underdeveloped.

Produces Low Percentage of Good Players

One of the biggest problems in a competitive system is that far too few players or participants really develop high-level skills or the emotional maturity that true mastery requires. Let me give an example from my own experience. I have been teaching tennis to high-school boys and girls for thirty years. Surprisingly, I have observed that less than 10 percent become genuinely good players. The first reason for this is that most participants play tennis only during the high-school tennis season. Perhaps one-third play a little during the rest of the year. The majority are too busy with other sports, other activities, or schoolwork to find the time to play all year.

It is hard to excel at something when you don't maintain a consistent regimen. But in my experience, the main reason for mediocrity is that these kids are focused on winning before they have acquired the skills to play well. Some play for their school teams for four years, yet remain mediocre. It doesn't have to be this way. It is the same with many team sports; there are a few stars, and the rest of the players just fill positions.

This tendency toward mediocrity doesn't just apply to children. I have been teaching and observing adult tennis players for nearly forty years. Most people who play the game for many years don't improve that much. They tend to plateau and stay at the same level no matter how many years they play. The reason is simple. Most people who play tennis go out on the court, warm up for ten minutes, and start competing. They don't practice their basic skills; they just play matches. Playing this way ingrains poor physical, mental and emotional habits that limit their potential. They think they are only going to improve by competing, yet they never make much progress, and they don't understand why. This tendency toward a minority of excellence and a majority of mediocrity occurs in almost every area of endeavor where competition reigns, from school to sports to business to politics.

Beats Down the Naturals

Wanting to do our best is a noble goal. But the side effects of a competitive system significantly diminish our chances of attaining this goal. The people we compete against do everything in their power to keep us from doing our best. They want to beat us. They don't want us to play our best—unless they still win. This is how the competitive system works.

Some people are naturally gifted; certain abilities come more easily to them. In our competitive system, people with less natural talent are encouraged to do whatever it takes to beat the more naturally talented people. This may include questionable tactics, such as physical or psychological intimidation; or even cheating. When someone has a natural gift, it would be wise to fully support their development as they have the potential to raise the bar to higher levels. But this is not what is promoted in a competitive system.

Some of these "naturals" however, also do their best to beat down and lower the confidence of the less talented, thereby hindering them from attaining their potential. Such behavior is subtly and at times overtly encouraged in the competitive system. And it is often interpreted as a sign of having the will or toughness to succeed. But it exacts a tremendous price on both winners and losers, on the naturally talented as well as those less gifted. Ultimately we all miss out through the potential that is never fulfilled, and the shining examples who might have been.

Precludes Relaxed Focus

People do develop focus when thrown prematurely into competition; but it is the focus of a startled rabbit. It's natural to be scared when we aren't sure if we know what we are doing, or whether we will be able to perform when it counts. With our ego and self-esteem on the line, our focus is distorted by tension. We go on a high alert, fight-or-flight mode that is not conducive to a relaxed focus or to peak performance. Performance anxiety obstructs the relaxed focus that produces the highest level of skill.

Discourages Physical Fitness

One of the worst side effects of over-emphasizing competition in the learning process is that many people develop an aversion to exercise and athletics. In school, children are at times forced to exercise and compete in ways that are stressful, not fun. Not surprisingly, many develop an aversion to exercise and sports. Physical Education can become a miserable chore for those who don't do well in competitive environments, especially when they have learned to see themselves as losers from their earliest experiences. I believe this to be a factor in our current epidemic of obesity. Ask most people with a weight problem about their experiences in school physical education programs and organized athletics, and you will hear a litany of tales of woe.

Increases Self-inflicted Injuries

Another liability arising from the premature introduction of competition in sports is that habitual repetition of incorrect physical mechanics increases the chances of injury. An improperly performed mechanical action – a pitch in baseball or a serve in tennis – irritates and stresses muscles and joints. Such an action, repeated over and over, often leads to injury. It is a version of the well-known repetitive stress syndrome. Developing skill requires mastering proper form, which allows our actions to be more efficient and comparatively effortless. When we start competing prematurely, we shift our focus from skill development to winning however we can; and proper form is usually the first casualty.

Competitive sports, especially at higher levels, require exercise and conditioning to excel. At all levels, from recreational to professional, overuse is a significant issue, particularly for less naturally talented players. The only way to make up for a lack of talent is to train harder. And intense training takes its toll on our bodies. We accept as inevitable that our joints are going to break down as we age. But this "natural" event is greatly hastened if we push our bodies too hard. Look at the number of ex-athletes, from ballet dancers to football players, who can barely walk later in life. Pushing ourselves to extremes to compete is detrimental to our health.

Triggers Performance Anxiety

In a competitive society we are often expected or told to "be confident" even before we know what we are doing. It's good to have confidence in our ability to learn. But how can we be confident, especially in competition, before we've really learned the basic skills? True confidence doesn't come from false bravado, but from hard-earned proficiency and the knowledge that we have the skills necessary to succeed. And whether we're children or adults, when we haven't developed these skills, that little voice inside us knows, and tells us, that we don't know what we're doing.

Performance anxiety occurs when we're put into competition before developing a deep inner confidence in our skills and ourselves. If we haven't adequately developed the necessary physical, mental, and emotional skills in a cooperative environment, it's almost impossible to develop secure confidence or perform at our highest level in competition. There's always another contest and even if we won the last one, there's still someone wanting to beat us in the next one, and the next, and the next. Watch people compete at any level, in any endeavor, and you will often see performance anxiety manifest. Experienced competitors are often better at dealing with or masking their anxiety, but even the best often tighten up or "choke" when the pressure is on.

In general, everyone has some performance anxiety potential, even five- and six-year-olds. It seems to be a natural aspect of the human condition, and it may be connected to our innate fight-or-flight response, hardwired in the limbic brain. But I have come to the conclusion that most of performance anxiety is artificially induced. It only seems natural in a highly competitive culture where nearly everyone is thrust prematurely into competitive situations.

Early experiences of failing or losing under pressure etch the first traces of performance anxiety deep within our emotional cellular memory, and in our subconscious mind. Present performance anxiety is intrinsically related to past experiences of failure in learning or performance situations. And once this anxiety is ingrained in our cellular memory, it often remains as an inhibiting response to perceived pressure long after we stop competing.

Induces Choking

Choking is the ultimate expression of performance anxiety. Sports provide the clearest examples of choking, but it occurs in all areas of life. In 1993, tennis professional Jana Novotna, lost a match she was dominating in the finals at Wimbledon. She was about to ascend to the pinnacle of tennis, when she missed an easy shot. She started thinking about that error and ended up "losing it," missing shot after shot, including several easy ones.

After the match, she was crying on the Duchess of Kent's shoulder. Novotna was one of the best players in the world at the time, and yet she completely choked and lost all confidence in her skills. This response was the result of previous experiences earlier in her life. (She eventually redeemed herself by winning Wimbledon in 1998.) This is not an atypical example. In fact, it is quite common.

The 2005 U.S. Open Women's Golf Championships was more of a Greek battlefield than a golf tournament. Annika Sorenstam dramatically blew her chance to win her third major tournament of the year on the way to winning the grand slam (all four majors for the year). No player, man or woman, has ever won all four of golf's major championships in one year. Having won the first two majors that year, Sorenstam was heavily favored to win this tournament also. But with all the hype around her possibly winning golf's grand slam, she tightened up and choked it away.

In the same tournament, Paula Creamer and Michelle Wie, two of golf's new stars, also choked their chances of a title. At the top of the leader board going into the final round – Wie in the lead and Creamer one stroke behind – by the end of the day Creamer had gone eight strokes over par and Wie was eleven over. Lorena Ochoa, in the same tournament, was two strokes out of the lead until, at the last hole, she shot a quadruple bogey eight and dropped far out of contention.

In October that same year another top pro golfer, John Daly, about to win a pro tournament in San Francisco, missed two three-foot putts and fell by the wayside. These disastrous chokes are common to professionals in every competitive field. Again, it can be argued that even at the highest levels, more competitions are lost rather than won.

Choking is not due to some mysterious "fatal flaw" in our character, but to patterns etched into our cellular memory through past experiences in competitive situations for which we were truly unprepared. In our culture, we are all put into competition before we have learned the mental and emotional skills to keep us from choking. Put in situations too advanced for our skill level, before we have mastered the fundamentals, we make inevitable critical mistakes that mark us as "losers". Such common scenarios, repeated over time, program deep inner self-doubts into our cellular memory that often prevent us from performing at our full potential.

Motivates Through External Rewards

To compete, most people require some form of external reward, even if it is only the recognition of being the winner. This starts off innocently enough in children's games where we are often bribed to compete; offered a soda or some paltry reward if we are the winner. Early on in school, we often compete for a teacher's gold stars. From there it goes on – the quest for A's in school, trophies in sports, big bonuses in business, and status in society.

In America it is increasingly difficult to motivate children without offering some external reward. They often want to know what they are going to get before agreeing to do what you ask them to do, having been conditioned to respond this way by virtually every aspect of society. This is prevalent in school, in athletics, and at home. Parents often motivate children to perform tasks, from cleaning their rooms to doing their homework, by offering some form of reward.

In my tennis program, some children have asked me what are they going to get if they do what I'm asking. I tell them they're going to become good tennis players, but that is usually not the answer they're looking for. This aspect of the competitive system – using external rewards (bribes) as motivation – results in many children losing the ability to motivate themselves simply for the enjoyment of doing the activity itself. They become conditioned to expect external rewards.

This mercenary mentality has also contaminated the world of professional sports. How many professional athletes would put in the countless hours of grueling training and work if there were no giant carrot dangling in front of them? Many athletes are now more consumed with the carrot than with the love of their game. It is arguably the same in almost every competitive industry, from sports, to the arts, to technology and business. When external rewards and punishments become the main motivators in any game or contest, the competitors become mercenaries.

Fosters Overwork

Americans work harder, and longer, with less enjoyment, than citizens in most other developed countries. Many people do become highly successful in our competitive system, often at the expense of a healthy and balanced character and personal life. Successful people must work hard to maintain their lifestyle. Sixty to eighty hour weeks are not uncommon in many top professional echelons. (It takes a lot of effort to make a lot of money and then keep track of it.) Desire for material rewards and prestige, and fear of failure are less-than-optimal motivations. As primary motivations, they don't produce psychological health or the best long-term results in the development of character.

On the other end of the economic scale, the poor, and increasingly the middle-class, must work as hard, or harder, just to survive, pay for their homes and raise their children. Many work two or three jobs, sixty or more hours a week at minimum wage. Whether rich or poor, most people are constantly on the go, trying to get ahead within our competitive system. The weekly schedule of any family includes one activity after another, from the moment they wake up to the minute they go to bed. Weekends often cram as many fun activities into two days as possible, and frequently include children's sporting events or performances. There is little time for the downtime so vital for our overall development and well being; the time when we can quietly contemplate the bigger questions of existence and get perspective on our own life or the world at large.

Provokes Conflict

Competition can elicit camaraderie through teamwork, but it also stimulates and provokes conflict. In subtle and not so subtle ways, we are taught to cooperate with and respect the players on our team, and to regard the other side as enemies. Yet even among teammates there is a constant battle to get ahead. We often compete against our teammates for a chance to stand in the lineup or get more playing time. Camaraderie, team spirit, and bonding reside in constant tension with the competitive desire to be number one.

As in war, to see our opponents as human beings is considered weakness. It diminishes the "killer attitude" so highly regarded in competition. This explains why verbal aggression and trash talk are rampant in sports. Look at the common sports vocabulary. We "beat the hell out of," "crush," "destroy," and "kill" our opponents. We call them bums or losers, pussies or faggots, to anger and distract them and lower their self-confidence. Many players frequently taunt their own teammates in the same fashion.

The higher the stakes, the greater the frequency and intensity of such hostile/aggressive behavior. Examples include late hits in football, cheap shots in hockey and basketball, and baseball pitchers purposely trying to hit batters in order to intimidate them. And legendary race car driver, Dale Earnhardt, was called The Intimidator for good reason.

We have all seen reports on the correlation between aggressiveness in athletics being tied to aggressive behavior outside the athletic arena. This behavior is not coincidental. Our competitive system exerts ever-increasing pressure to win on people at higher levels. Where does it end? How many hours can someone work or practice? How much stress can someone endure without cracking? How much needless stress is added by an imbalanced emphasis on winning, and an unhealthy scorn for losing? Perhaps a more cooperative, excellence oriented focus in the early stages of learning would allow us all to accomplish a lot more, with a lot less stress.

Tacitly Encourages Cheating

Cheating is commonplace in a competitive system. We have all witnessed this behavior many times. In May 2005, Tarrin, one of my tennis students, went to Mexico to play in three entry-level professional tennis tournaments. If you win enough matches in these tournaments the results count toward attaining a world ranking. This was Tarrin's first experience at this level.

In these tournaments, players without a ranking have to play in a pre-qualifying tournament before getting into the main draw. In these pre-qualifying matches there are no line judges to determine whether a ball is in or out, so the players are responsible for making their own calls. In tennis, you get to call the balls on your side of the net and the other player has to accept your call. If you doubt the veracity of the other player, you can request that someone come and watch the lines and rule on any disputed calls.

In Tarrin's first match, her opponent cheated on the first three points — in the first game! Her opponent was sending the message that she was going to do anything to win. After her experiences at these tournaments, Tarrin concluded that this behavior was the rule rather than the exception. She likened the girls and their coaches to sharks in a feeding frenzy. The protocol seemed to be that if other players cheated you, you just cheated them right back.

Even signing up for practice courts was illustrative: If you signed up for a court in pencil instead of pen, when you came back the next day you found that your name had been erased and someone else had signed in with a pen. This is a sad statement on the current state of competitive sports — and this in the relatively civilized game of tennis! Imagine what is happening in other sports!

The reality is that our current competitive system tacitly encourages cheating. There is much talk of fairness and playing by the rules, and many coaches and players do abide by the rules. However, there are more than a few coaches who teach their players to bend the rules and try to get away with what they can.

Leo Durocher, the legendary former manager of baseball's Los Angeles Dodgers, once said, "What are we at the park for except to win? I'd trip my mother. I'd help her up, brush her off, and tell her I'm sorry. But my mother wouldn't make it to third." An announcer for the 2006 World Cup stated, "There is no such thing as cheating in soccer, we just bend the rules until they break." People don't like to acknowledge this behavior, but it is going on everywhere there is a competition.

Coaches with an "anything goes" attitude teach their athletes that, in order to win, they need every advantage. The message is, "If you don't get caught, it's good because it will increase our chances of winning." This mindset is connected to the steroid scandals that plague nearly every sport, with the possible exception of lawn bowling! It is telling that of the many players caught using steroids, it's hard to think of one who has expressed regret for their behavior. Most justify this illegal form of performance enhancement by saying that the practice is so widespread they have to do it just to stay competitive!

Institutionalizes Injustice

"It is a curious race indeed in which one competitor must try to scramble up from poverty while another starts out with a huge trust fund." Alfie Kohn

It is a truism in life that the winners make the rules, and the rules generally increase the advantage of the "winners" and the disadvantage of the "losers". This brings up another negative aspect of the competitive system: It promotes institutionalized injustice, including racism, poverty and socio-economic class divisions. This unjust advantage/disadvantage dynamic permeates education, business, politics, international relations, and history. In education, the lion's share of funding goes to well-to-do neighborhoods and even private schools, while poor inner-city schools are given scraps from the table.

Large corporate chain stores increasingly move into neighborhoods, drive small family-run or privately owned businesses out of business, and remove the profits and benefits out of those communities to corporate headquarters and the bank accounts of grossly overpaid CEO's. Meanwhile, independent political candidates with original ideas are unable to compete with "mainstream" candidates funded by corporate special interest lobbies to whom they are beholden once elected. And third world countries, continually exploited economically by "first world" nations, remain in poverty generation after generation. All such inequities, hallmarks of the competitive system, inhibit initiative, and severely limit the availability and free flow of new ideas and solutions both to and from the disadvantaged sectors. In this way, injustices are institutionalized, and we all miss out on the chance to benefit from the creativity and excellence of millions of people.

Microsoft founder Bill Gates, in a commencement speech at a high-school graduation, listed some rules of life that he found important. Of course those "rules" largely reflected the competitive mindset that made him one of the richest entrepreneurs on the planet. His first rule: "Life is not fair — get used to it!" No one can argue with the first part of this statement; we have all witnessed firsthand how unfair life can be. But a better end to his statement might have been, "Let's see what we can do about it!"

WHAT LESSONS ARE WE TEACHING?

The positive virtues of competition have always been promoted, while the behavioral problems that emerge when we throw people into competition before they have developed the necessary skills to be successful, have been downplayed as a necessary evil. All the issues cited in this chapter, all the negative behaviors that appear in a competitive system in which winning is the bottom line, are reason enough to reevaluate how we learn, and how and when we compete. What are we teaching, and encouraging, when we make winning paramount? Aren't we tacitly encouraging competitors to do whatever it takes, and whatever they think they can get away with, to succeed?

Deception, lying, intimidation, abuse, and increasingly in sports, illegal steroid use for physical enhancement, are commonly used to increase the chances of winning. Such unethical tactics are widely accepted as winning strategies not only in sports, but also in business, politics, public debates, relationships, and even religion. Consider trash talking radio and TV "shock jocks", dirty, mud-slinging tactics by political candidates, and threats of hell, damnation and even death by fundamentalist and fanatical religionists. At the middle to upper levels in sports, business, or politics, the constant jockeying for material rewards and position in the pecking order tends to increase such abusive and aberrant behaviors. By rewarding the most competitive and aggressive behavior, we reinforce that behavior. Thus our competitive system inflicts wide-ranging corrosive effects and ingrains deep and disturbing patterns that manifest everywhere in life. These behaviors and patterns represent our "canaries in the coalmine." signaling us that we need to change course.

WHAT CAN WE DO?

How do we keep children from learning to lie, cheat, steal, and intimidate when they see so many famous, important, and respected people doing it — and getting away with it? Whether in business, politics, sports, journalism, academics, or religion someone always seems to be trying to get ahead by bending the rules. In business, industry, politics, or law, it is increasingly not called cheating, it's just "gaming the system," taking advantage wherever you can. Winning and the rewards of winning are the bottom line in today's competitive system, and this reality tests people's moral fiber—especially if they haven't developed the skills to succeed, and the maturity needed to handle both success and failure.

Many people attribute lying, cheating, and stealing to the "bad apples" in society, or they say people are inherently weak and unethical. This may be true for a small percentage of people. But most people are basically good. I believe a competitive system that prizes winning above excellence and ethics subtly condones "bad" behavior. When the pressure is on, a significant percentage of people will do whatever they need to do to come out ahead.

In order to protect the competitive system, its proponents tend to deflect criticism away from the system's underlying problems, and toward the individuals within the system who act out and make visible those underlying problems. They scapegoat the "bad apples" instead of recognizing and addressing the underlying flaws in the system that helps to create those apples. If the system didn't tacitly encourage and reward unethical behavior, such behavior wouldn't be so pervasive. And we might not need all the rules outlawing these behaviors.

It's hard to see how to change such widespread and deeply

entrenched problems and behaviors, especially when we believe they are just part of human nature. But once we recognize and acknowledge the unhealthy aspects of the competitive system that spawns these problems and behaviors, we can begin solving them by making appropriate changes in the system itself. It is essential to encourage a high level of personal ethics and accountability. But it is equally important to hold accountable a system that places so much importance and pressure on winning at all costs.

No system can legitimately teach the highest ethical standards while tacitly supporting, encouraging, or tolerating such behavior. Do these bottom-line values that presently pervade our competitive system hold the brightest promise for our future? Are these the values we want to promote and pass on to our children? These are the kinds of questions we need to begin to ask, as individuals and as a society.

I suggest that we can achieve far better results and promote more effective learning and behaviors by applying non-competitive principles. I believe that a non-competitive approach offers a way out of our current competitive morass. A non-competitive learning system emphasizes mastering basic skills and developing emotional maturity before competition, and simultaneously emphasizing internal rewards – the enjoyment of an activity and of the learning process for their own sakes – while de-emphasizing external rewards. This approach diminishes negative behaviors like lying, cheating, and intimidation.

Change the system and behavior will change also. Because such behaviors have been so deeply engrained in many people's cellular memory, it will take time for these behaviors to disappear in those who have been raised in our highly competitive system. But a new generation will thrive in a system of excellence-based non-competitive education. We will begin to explore this new model in the next chapter.

> *If we don't change the direction we are headed,*
> *we will end up where we are going.*
> —Chinese proverb

PART TWO
Beyond Competition

When an archer is shooting for nothing,
He has all his skill.
If he shoots for a brass buckle,
He is already nervous.
If he shoots for a prize of gold,
He goes blind
Or sees two targets —
He is out of his mind!

His skill has not changed,
But the prize
Divides him. He cares.
He thinks more of winning
Than of shooting —
And the need to win
Drains him of power.
— Chuang Tzu

3
Birth of a Non-competitive Model

There is a road
No simple highway
Between the dawn
and the dark of night
And if you go
no one may follow
That path is for
your steps alone.

— Robert Hunter

More than forty years' involvement in sports and education has allowed me to see the competitive learning system "up close and personal". Like many small town boys growing up in the 1960s, I played a variety of sports, including baseball, basketball and tennis. These activities were competitive from the start. We would practice as a team for a few weeks, and then start competing against each other and then other teams. While our practices included some drilling of the fundamentals, they revolved mainly around competition. Even the drills often involved some form of competition.

When I started playing tennis at the age of fourteen, it was the same routine. The coach showed us the basic strokes, taught us how to keep score, let us practice a little while, and almost immediately started us playing matches. As you can imagine, I was programming plenty of less-than-optimal habits into my cellular memory. I did very well in high-school tennis, winning over 90 percent of my matches at the number two singles position in my last three years, and going undefeated my senior season, but this was nowhere close to my potential. It would be many more years before I discovered another way.

PLAYING IN THE ZONE

A big factor in my developing the non-competitive teaching system I call *Effortless Tennis*, which draws on the principles of what I call *Effortless Learning*, came out of my desire as a tennis player to get into and stay in the fabled state known as *the zone*, that magical place where everything comes together, and we play "out of our minds". When we are in the zone, everything goes right and nothing goes wrong. It is as if we can't make a mistake. This is "peak performance".

Athletes generally long for the Zone, but rarely attain it. Yet musicians and dancers frequently enter the zone. This is because music and dance are taught through a more non-competitive, cooperative, skill-based approach that allows greater access to the zone. Musicians and dancers are supposed to work together. The zone exists for any endeavor, be it cooking, knitting, writing, driving, managing, accounting, even living. Dr. Martin Luther King, Jr.'s "I have a dream" speech is a shining example of the zone.

I began exploring this phenomenon in 1974 after several experiences of being in the zone. I wanted to know more about it so I could experience it more frequently. Tennis pro and sports psychologist Tim Gallwey's seminal book, *The Inner Game of Tennis*, published that same year, provided a catalyst that deepened my interest in the zone. Gallwey, a pioneer in illuminating the importance of mental and psychological skills in sports, showed that our biggest challenge to achieving success on a consistent basis lies between our ears — in our mind. Remember that in 1974 not much attention had been focused on psychological development in sports. Now, sports psychology is an integral part of any training program, but before 1974 hardly anyone talked about it.

Gallwey noted that the ego, or as he called it, Self 1, wants to control everything we do. Like a know-it-all, it constantly chatters in our head, analyzing, judging and criticizing our every move. This mental chatter distracts our focus on present activities, making it impossible to do our best, and harder to attain our goals. Our subconscious, or Self 2, is where we are able to perform tasks without having to think about them. The challenge is learning how to master and transcend our mind instead of letting it work against us. We need to learn to keep Self 1 occupied while we perform. Gallwey talked a lot about learning to trust our body. "Only when we succeed at quieting Self 1 — the conscious, thinking, egoistic mind — does the true potential of the human body begin to show itself," Gallwey wrote. Our true potential lies in the zone where we play "out of our mind" in a truly effortless fashion.

TRYING TOO HARD

Gallwey's *Inner Tennis* helped me to understand a common obstacle to attaining the zone and therefore peak performance. That obstacle is the idea of "trying too hard." So often I had heard coaches exhorting players to "Try harder!" "C'mon, you're not trying hard enough!" One of my beginning students recently shared a traumatic experience she had when she was eight years old, when her coach yelled at her, in front of two hundred people, that she wasn't trying hard enough. "No wonder I never wanted to participate in sports!" she said. Through her practice of Effortless Tennis, she's become a good athlete. Imagine if she had been taught this way from the start.

Most people think that if we just put in more effort and keep trying harder, we will succeed. But this is not how it works. A clear example of trying too hard is when we watch young children in a footrace. Most are producing great effort; their faces contorted, their muscles seized up, but they aren't moving very fast. Interestingly, I see this same response when people first come to play tennis. People are trying too hard and not getting very far. When we are already trying hard, trying harder makes us physically tense and emotionally uptight, dramatically lowering our performance and our enjoyment. Trying too hard bars our access to the zone.

COMPETITION AS AN IMPEDIMENT TO THE ZONE

After many years studying the zone, I started realizing that the biggest obstacle to attaining this elusive state wasn't our lack of ability, but, once again, the premature introduction of competition into the learning process. Psychology professor, Mihaly Csikszentmihalyi, in his well-known book *Flow*, buttresses this realization: "Competitive sports are less conducive to the flow experience than non-competitive activities." When we lack confidence in our skills, we are too tense about our performance to relax into the zone. Being in the zone cannot be forced. Trying harder never gets us there.

The higher our level of skill development, the closer we are to excellence, and the easier it is to enter the zone. Being in the zone is both a high-skill experience and, paradoxically, a seemingly effortless one. We may glimpse the zone at earlier points in our development. But only when we have mastered fundamental skills and are able to consistently perform at a high level can we experience the zone on a regular basis.

My observations over the years indicate that, for most people, developing the skills to consistently enter the zone requires freedom from the negative effects produced by the premature introduction of competition into the learning process. First achieving excellence and healthy self-confidence prepares us to compete, and grants more consistent access to the zone, even in competition.

After decades of studying this phenomenon, I am convinced that the zone is our natural state. But we have been taken out of, and denied access to our natural state by the premature introduction of competition. Non-competitive learning prepares us to enter the zone as a natural, even inevitable phase of the learning process. By not rushing people into competition, we are able to learn the skills and develop the confidence, which are a passport into the zone. It is not magic, although it feels like it when we're there. It is a simple shift in focus from winning to learning, and from competing to self-mastery.

THE BEGINNINGS OF EFFORTLESS LEARNING

In January 1982, I took a less-than-successful trip — at least in competitive terms — to New Zealand to play in a series of professional satellite tennis tournaments. Before returning to the United States, I decided to take a few days for a side trip to Waiheke Island, thirty miles off the coast. I was staying in a youth hostel and feeling quite low because I hadn't won many matches. I decided to take a hike to explore the island. Noticing a beautiful peninsula jutting far out into the water, I made up my mind to hike to the very tip.

I walked across classic New Zealand sheep-filled fields and started following the peninsula out into the water. The land grew narrower and gradually more elevated. After walking for over an hour I reached a point where the land rose several hundred feet above the ocean and turned to jagged rocks. The day had been quite sunny, but as I began scaling the rocks, the wind picked up, blowing gray clouds rapidly overhead. Halfway up the rocky ascent, I realized that my situation had become dangerous. But I kept climbing. My hike became a metaphor for my life. I felt I had to make it to the end of the peninsula, that if I couldn't conquer the challenge of my rocky journey, I was destined to be a failure. My little hike had taken on profound significance.

Spurred on and determined in the face of my recent losses, I pushed on. The climb grew increasingly dangerous, and I became scared. Finally I said to myself, "It's not worth it." I turned and went back to a safe location and sat down on a large rock overlooking the water. Now I was really depressed. I hadn't achieved my goal. As I sat there contemplating my life, wondering where it was going, an idea suddenly flashed into my mind. "Maybe there's another way that isn't as dangerous that will allow me to reach my goal." I returned to a lower point on the rocky hill and, sure enough, I discovered an animal trail that led safely and effortlessly around the dangerous part, giving me easy access to my destination. I credit this experience with allowing me to see that there are many paths to achieving the same goal, and that achieving our goals doesn't require us to jeopardize our lives. This was my first conscious glimpse of the concept of effortlessness. The insight I gained from this experience strongly influenced how I began to approach playing and teaching tennis, and eventually, living my life.

In the summer of 1987 I changed the name of my tennis program from *Tennis for the Body, Mind, and Spirit* to *Effortless Tennis*. In my years of watching and participating in athletics, I had personally experienced the zone while playing tennis, and also seen many athletes reach this state. One of the most common adjectives athletes used to describe these peak experiences was *effortless*. This was also my experience. Effortless Tennis was indeed the perfect name for my program.

Some people initially misinterpret my use of *effortless*. I am not saying learning is easy, or that it requires no effort to achieve a goal. The word *effortless* points to a relaxed and aware focus we bring to learning basic skills and developing mastery, free of the stressful distractions of premature competition. Learning this way ingrains a relaxed and aware focus in our cellular memory. It prepares us to perform as effortlessly as possible at our highest potential, and helps us achieve our long-term goals.

We do not begin learning effortlessly. Much physical, mental, and emotional development is required to learn any skill. But any skill that we have mastered becomes relatively easy – *effortless*. Through mastery we more easily enter the zone where we perform at peak levels without self-conscious effort. Our cellular memory does it for us. With all the elements patterned into our subconscious, our skill *is* effortless. We seem to be doing so little as we function at our peak; and at times we seem able to do the impossible.

ALFIE KOHN'S *NO CONTEST*

In October 1992 I read Alfie Kohn's landmark work entitled *No Contest: The Case against Competition*. Kohn's exhaustive research is impressive, and his conclusions are compelling. His research lays to rest all claims that a competitive learning system is superior to a system based on cooperation.

Kohn exposes the heavy costs of our competitive system, and urges us to move in a more cooperative direction. The thrill of victory and the agony of defeat are real; but there is far more agony than thrills for most of us in our current competitive system. This is due to what Kohn calls "mutually exclusive goal attainment," – i.e. in any contest, only one person or team can win. Ergo, *I* can't win unless *you* lose. This dynamic puts winning at a premium.

No Contest had a monumental impact on my life. Although I had been moving toward a non-competitive model for many years, it inspired me to create a more cooperative method of teaching and learning, and ultimately served as the catalyst for my removing all competition from my tennis program. I wrote *Evolutionary Education* hoping to refocus attention on this important subject. If you wish to explore this subject further, I highly recommend *No Contest*, as well as Kohn's follow-up book, *Punished by Rewards*. (See the Recommended Resources section at the end of this book.)

The Kumon Method: The 100 Percent Solution

The Kumon method also provided me with insights that helped me develop Effortless Tennis and Effortless Learning. Kumon, a system of learning developed in Japan in 1958, started as a method for teaching mathematics, and was adapted to teaching languages. It is comprised of a series of many exams ranging from the most basic to the most advanced levels of subject material. In the Kumon system, the only way a student can advance to the next exam is to get 100 percent on the previous exam. Not 99 percent — 100 percent! So long as the subject material is identified accurately, this method offers a sure path to mastery.

Some people feel that expecting 100 percent is too much to ask of students. In America, we allow students to pass with a grade of 70 percent or even less. But consider that a 70 percent score means a student doesn't understand 30 percent of the material, virtually one-third! 90 percent means they don't know 10 percent of the material. This could be a big problem if that 10 percent includes information essential to understanding the next level of a subject. (What 10 percent of knowledge would you be comfortable with your surgeon, or your dentist, or the pilot flying your airplane, not knowing?) The Kumon system understands that a 10 percent lack of mastery of the basics will inhibit a student's development at the next level. Requiring 100 percent to move forward ensures that they develop the fundamental skills that enable them to grasp and learn the more advanced levels. The Kumon focus is on mastery, not competition.

The lack of a valid method for determining whether children have mastered the basics before they move ahead, and the additional emphasis on competition even before mere proficiency is attained, is a key factor in the decline of our educational system. We give children too much information and too little time to digest and comprehend it, and present even more advanced material before they have truly learned and incorporated the previous material.

Over the years I have heard countless people say that they studied certain material for a test, and afterward couldn't remember the material. Students study for an exam, memorize rather than truly comprehend the material, and then forget much of what they learned. Of course the utility of getting 100 percent on a test before moving on depends on the tests being well designed and covering relevant material. We have all taken tests where we were required to memorize obscure facts that really weren't worth retaining.

The value of requiring 100 percent learning of materials is that it emphasizes and virtually ensures mastery at each level of the learning process as far as we choose to go in that subject. This profoundly effective approach to learning eliminates the conventional striving for grades in that students are working for a 100 percent grasp of a subject, rather than competing with each other for a better grade.

This doesn't mean that we have to learn every subject to its highest level of mastery, but we should be proficient in the fundamentals. Not everyone needs to know advanced calculus, but everyone benefits from being able to add, subtract, multiply, and divide. Not everyone needs to know five languages, but it would seem reasonable to be able to read, write, and converse intelligently in our native tongue. Imagine if all students truly mastered all of the fundamentals of all of their subjects, and achieved the highest levels of mastery in their chosen fields. The world would be a very different place indeed! But even the Kumon approach cannot be truly non-competitive if it is taught within a highly competitive system. The competitive system itself will still need to be changed.

MASTERING THE BASICS FIRST

After digesting the Kumon approach to learning, I applied its central idea — the importance of mastering the fundamentals before moving to the next level — when teaching my students. In Effortless Tennis and Effortless Learning, students start out each day doing the same exercises they did the last time they were on court or in the classroom. If they are making mistakes with the most basic drills, they are not ready to move on to the more advanced skills. This approach has proven to be invaluable to the learning progression of my students. Practicing the basic skills to the point of proficiency before moving to the next level of skill development gives them a strong foundation in the fundamentals, and a corresponding level of confidence and self-esteem.

Working on the basics to the point of mastery results in far greater retention of the material in any subject. Most American children have experienced this by singing "The Alphabet Song" over and over to the point of mastery, when the song is forever ingrained in their cellular memory!

FROM NON-ATHLETE TO ATHLETE

One of my most important personal experiences of witnessing the benefits of mastering the basics first occurred in the late 1980s and early 1990s. John, a high-school student, began taking private tennis lessons with me, and coming to my junior clinics regularly. I worked with John in his last three years of high school. John was a great kid — intelligent, laid-back, non-athletic and not very competitive. There was little chance that John, given his temperament, background, and level of coordination, would succeed in competitive sports. His desire, willpower, and self-esteem would have been crushed long before he developed the necessary skills.

This almost happened anyway. Some of John's teammates were very hard on him during the first two years teasing him that he looked good, but he couldn't win. Even his coach put pressure on him because he wasn't winning. John got very discouraged after the second year because of this taunting, but I assured him that from where he began his development, he would need another year for all his skills to come together. Fortunately, he trusted me and stayed with it.

One of my friends, who had been in the Effortless Tennis program for several years also became John's mentor, and adopted him as his practice partner. For a couple of years they practiced at least twice a week, sometimes more, doing all the drills necessary for John to learn and master the fundamental skills. In keeping with the effortless model, they didn't play games for points. This allowed John to develop the physical, mental, and emotional skills he needed to be able to play the game well. I also worked with the top six singles players on the team for those three years, shifting their focus from competing to developing their physical, mental, and emotional skills in a non-competitive setting.

The results speak for themselves. John went from being the last player on the team his freshman year to being number three his senior year. His team went from a record of one win and thirteen losses to an undefeated season and winner of the county team championship, something that hadn't happened in over twenty-five years.

I have worked with many other students who started out with very poor coordination. As I discovered, this was often not due to lack of ability, but lack of opportunity to develop their skills in a nurturing, non-competitive environment. If people stay with an Effortless Learning program, their skills begin to develop. This usually takes around a year for people with limited coordination. But often, those who take longer to develop, when given the opportunity to do so, end up developing the furthest and producing the most amazing results in the long run.

MENTAL AND EMOTIONAL COMPONENTS

Many people mistakenly believe that physical skills are basic skills, while mental and emotional skills are more advanced skills. Nothing could be further from the truth. Consider this: If we have poor concentration while learning, and fail to develop our concentration as we practice "basic" skills, we will be programming poor concentration into our cellular memory. If we regularly experience anxiety, uncertainty, or fear while learning a chosen skill, yet fail to develop the skills of relaxation and calmness, we will be programming unhealthy and distracting emotions into our cellular memory. Such emotions will then be triggered automatically as we engage in that activity. They will be ingrained responses occurring outside our conscious control. The fear of public speaking is a common example for many people. But even deeply ingrained emotional patterns can be changed or positively reprogrammed as we go back and master the fundamentals through Effortless Learning.

This is true in my own experience. In elementary school, I started playing the drums and played in the school band throughout high school. Unfortunately, I didn't learn some of the fundamentals of music and drumming, so I was often a bit anxious while drumming.

After high school, I stopped drumming for ten years, except for tapping on the steering wheel, table, or my knees. Then I started playing percussion with some friends in a band. My anxiety and uncertainty returned. After moving to California, I got into another band and started taking percussion lessons and going to African drum and dance classes and camps. Even after many years of working on my drumming, I never escaped that sense of uncertainty. Because of my childhood experiences, the uncertainty had become part of my cellular memory.

After taking competition out of my tennis program and recognizing the importance of mastering the basic skills, I finally realized a key source of my anxiety. There were some pieces of the fundamentals of rhythm and music that I still didn't understand. I started asking various teachers to show me the most basic fundamentals they knew. Over the course of several years, I discovered certain aspects of time and rhythmic patterns — fundamentals that I hadn't fully understood previously. These were the weak links that had been holding me back all those years.

Once I had discovered these missing links, I began to practice and embed them into my subconscious. As I did this, I noticed the feelings of anxiety and insecurity melting away. It took several years. Those old feelings still resurface once in a while, but not nearly as often, nor as intensely.

My experience has enabled me to help my students work through the same process. Rick came to my Effortless Tennis program in his forties. A good athlete, Rick had played competitive sports his whole life, and had acquired a host of deeply ingrained mental and emotional habits and reactions that severely limited his potential and his enjoyment of the games he played. He hadn't mastered the fundamentals of tennis, so we began working to pattern these basics into his cellular memory. At the same time we worked on re-patterning the "less than optimal" mental and emotional patterns that got in his way.

Rick got visibly upset whenever he missed almost any shot. Sometimes his reactions were so extreme I feared he might do himself bodily harm. Once this behavior started, it was virtually impossible to stop. He quickly lost self-control and the quality of his play went down the same slippery slope with his emotions. Playing poorly simply tore Rick apart. This behavioral pattern had dogged Rick for many years. By shifting the focus from competition and winning, to repetition for the purpose of developing competence, excellence, and mastery, Rick's deeply ingrained physical and emotional patterns and responses began to change for the better. Over a period of two to three years, Rick started to gain control over his emotional responses, and his game significantly improved.

Members of the club where Rick played noticed the changes in Rick. He was lighter, happier, and harder to beat. He didn't fall apart under the self-generated pressures of competition the way he used to. He had developed to the point where he almost didn't care if he won or lost. Tennis was no longer a game of life and death. It was a game of skill that he played for enjoyment. As a result, Rick began to win more than he lost. When club members asked him, "What happened to you?" Rick replied simply, "I've been learning how to play the game."

CHILDHOOD CONDITIONING

Many chronic negative mental, emotional and behavioral patterns are formed in childhood. For example, if we were able to get our way as children by being angry or sullen, or by acting out or crying, we likely experienced that behavior as successful, repeated it often, and patterned it into our cells over time. In time, such patterned behaviors become automatic character traits. And unless we consciously re-pattern new healthy behaviors, these old patterns will haunt us in some form for our entire lives.

Almost everyone struggles with various negative mental and emotional states ingrained in their cellular memories in childhood. These negative emotional patterns were often exacerbated by experiences within a competitive system. The learning process itself tends to trigger these emotions and behaviors.

In my experience 90 percent of the skills necessary for success in sports and movement activities are mental and emotional skills. The 10 percent of skills that are physical are extremely important, and are an integral part of the whole. If we don't develop fundamental mental and emotional skills, it takes us far longer to achieve proficiency in any endeavor, and often prevents us from attaining mastery. It also sours our experience of activities that ought to be enjoyable.

Mental and emotional skills are crucial and need to be developed from day one. They facilitate learning, making it easier and more enjoyable, which increases our chances of attaining excellence. If mental and emotional skills aren't taught from the beginning, less-than-optimal habits are patterned into our subconscious. It is much more difficult to change negative behavior patterns once they are ingrained in our cellular memory. This is why Effortless Learning places equal emphasis on mental, emotional and physical skills from the very beginning of the learning process.

THE IMPOSSIBLE DREAM?

Some of you may be thinking to yourselves, "It sounds great. But if we really had to master the fundamentals before competing, it might take years, or even a lifetime to get to the point where we are ready to compete." It might seem this way viewed from the perspective of the current competitive learning system. And this might in fact be the case for *some* people. But a non-competitive learning system dramatically increases the development of all the basic skills to the point of mastery. It then becomes a choice between achieving mastery in our chosen skill, or trying to become "winners" through premature competition, and postponing mastery in the process.

In Effortless Learning, each activity that we participate in allows us to work on our fundamental skills. We review and practice these basics to the point of proficiency before we move on to the next level. Many fundamental skills, especially mental and emotional skills, apply to all activities. So as we develop these skills in any activity, they carry over into most other activities.

When I teach my students the skills in Effortless Tennis, they discover that these skills are important to other activities that they are involved in, whether Aikido, bowling, dance, running a business, and even their relationships. Each activity may have its own unique set of fundamentals. But many of what I call the *Keys to Peak Performance* are central to all learning; they are universal. (I will describe these universal keys in greater depth in Chapter 6.)

As our skills become proficient, we can engage in competition — if we so desire. Until then, we focus on learning and mastering the basics, which can be very enjoyable and satisfying. When children learn this approach from the beginning, they naturally develop all of the key skills without the unpleasant stresses and emotions that are inevitable when premature competition is introduced. It is a natural and comparatively effortless progression. It won't take a lifetime to be ready to compete, if we so choose.

The Importance of Cellular Memory in the Learning Process

Teachers who understand and appreciate the fundamental importance of cellular memory to the physical, mental, and emotional aspects of the learning process can help us to achieve our full potential in any field. Let us take a closer look at how both positive and negative habits and patterns can be programmed into our cellular memory, helping us to learn and function effectively, or causing untold difficulties and problems.

From Repetition to Habit

Cellular memory can be a blessing or a curse, depending on whether good or poor physical and psychological habits and patterns are embedded in our cells. In tennis, every time we swing the racquet or move our body, the pattern of this movement leaves a biochemical imprint in the cells. Different chemicals react in different combinations to get our muscles to move. Every time an action is repeated, it reinforces the chemical imprint and the pattern becomes more deeply ingrained in our cellular memory.

After a certain amount of repetition, that action becomes a habit. Our body does the movement automatically; we don't have to think about it anymore. This is why it is so important to program desirable and efficient habits into our cellular memory from the beginning of our involvement in an activity. Once habits are formed, it is harder to make changes and adjustments, because these habits are etched in our cells, almost like encrypted software programs.

Unlearning poor habits is much more difficult than learning correctly from the start. In any activity, teaching efficient technique from the beginning is the most effective way to reach peak performance. With proper learning in a non-competitive environment we can ingrain skillful movements and habits and positive emotions into our cellular memory from the start. And those patterns will determine our instinctive reactions when we have no time to think. We will react with what works.

Cellular Reprogramming

I've worked with many individuals who had patterned unconscious inefficient movements and emotional reactions into their cellular memory. Competition prematurely introduced into the learning process is usually a significant factor. And I've learned that reprogramming good habits in place of poor habits is difficult if not impossible to achieve in the midst of competition.

When we make key changes to improve our game, our skill level tends to decline and we become virtual beginners for a period. Under the pressures of competition, we instinctively resort to old, ineffective habits and reactions. Such reprogramming is much easier in a cooperative learning environment, which is designed to help us slowly change our physical, mental, and emotional cellular memory. Even people with mild to severe learning problems are able to learn more efficiently, and begin making developmental leaps in a structured non-competitive environment.

The good news is that once we've patterned in optimal habits, they also are hard to change! The truism that once you learn how to ride a bicycle, you never forget, is true. I once taught a man in his late twenties who had been a ranked junior player in his teens. He hadn't played tennis in ten years. Yet thousands of hours of lessons, practice, junior clinics and tournaments had hard-wired his game into his subconscious. When he walked onto the court, the skills he had developed were at the level they had been ten years earlier. His entire game, his proper form and good habits, were indelibly etched into his cells, as were the areas that he hadn't fully developed.

ALL GOOD THINGS IN ALL GOOD TIME

As is now clear, the competitive system rushes us into competition long before we have mastered the basics. This obstructs and even sabotages the learning process. It fosters limiting physical and psychological habits and less than optimal performance. It diminishes our potential and our enjoyment of the activity, and may result in our giving up the activity altogether. Developing our full potential requires a nurturing, supportive, cooperative environment. Anything less will deliver less than our full potential.

When most of my adult students first arrive at the Effortless Tennis program, I see and feel a strong tension in them. They have been patterning this tension into their cellular memory, unknowingly, for decades. Most tend to experience psychological stress — uncertainty, self-doubt, anxiety, anger, fear, hyper-aggressive behavior, even sadness — while competing. They believe these emotional responses are an inherent part of competition, rather than evidence that they are not ready for competition. If you are experiencing these emotions you are not ready to compete. With children, the tension is there, but it is not as pronounced or as deeply ingrained. It's therefore much easier to work with children, and help them avoid this deep programming.

Almost anyone can learn to perform and even compete without these negative emotional patterns being programmed and then chronically triggered. The focus on developing our physical skills allows steady progression to the point of proficiency. This also develops our mental and emotional skills, which includes our confidence and self-esteem.

A good teacher can recognize when each student is *ready* to compete, and understands that not every student *has* to compete. Everyone is unique, and the appropriate time to compete is different for everyone. At some point, we may wish to compete to test our skills in a competitive arena and see how we handle the dynamics of competition.

A less psychologically healthy reason for wanting to compete is to prove to ourselves or someone else that we are worthy of respect. This is a frequent response from someone raised in a competitive environment. But we can fully engage most endeavors without competing as long as we wish, and continue to enjoy ourselves while developing and improving our skills. This is difficult to accomplish in our competitive system. But it is possible, especially once we make the shift to Effortless Learning.

THE RELIEF OF FINDING A NEW WAY

Many people who experience learning in a non-competitive environment notice a sense of psychological relief, as if a huge weight has been lifted off their shoulders. We've all grown up in a competitive system. Many of us have endured it without enjoying it — often because it felt like a lot of pressure and we weren't winning enough.

In the Effortless Learning program, people are able, often for the first time in their lives, to relax in a learning situation and experience what it's like to develop skills, competence and confidence without the familiar conditions of being pressured, judged or graded. But because many of us have internalized the competitive system due to our long-term immersion in it, it can take a while, sometimes years, to realize we aren't being judged, and to then stop judging ourselves as we learn and grow. Slowly but surely, we learn to relax and have fun, and our skills begin to improve at a faster rate. I have seen this happen with hundreds of people in the Effortless Tennis program.

After a while, people engaged in the process of Effortless Learning start to understand that it wasn't their laziness or lack of ability that prevented them from succeeding, but their lack of skill development. This lack of development may have occurred for several reasons: first, teachers weren't doing a good job explaining the fundamentals; second, teachers weren't giving students sufficient time and support to develop their skills before putting them into competition; third, the students put insufficient time and effort into learning the skills; and fourth, a combination of all of the above.

The Effortless Learning model addresses the above liabilities. I have seen no one fail who has stayed with the Effortless Learning process and put in the practice time. *Not one!* We need to give people encouragement and the time to learn all of the necessary skills. The last few decades have been an incredible journey for me. My experiences have completely changed how I understand and apply the learning process.

It is especially rewarding when I see people with deeply ingrained doubts about their ability to learn and succeed who really do want to learn, begin to believe and experience that it is possible for them to be good players. It shows in their eyes. It can take years between this moment of glimpsing our true potential, and actually fulfilling it. But many decide that it's worth sticking around for.

4
Advantages of Non-competitive Learning

When we know how to play the game,
success is the natural outcome.

I began deemphasizing competition in my teaching in the mid-1980s, and eliminated all competition from my program in 1992. Over the years, I have seen firsthand the extraordinary potential of this approach, not only for tennis but all types of education.

Most aspects of learning are similar in competitive and non-competitive learning systems. Many of the training methods are virtually identical. The fundamental skills are always the same. Both systems strive to make possible the achievement of competence, excellence and mastery by becoming proficient in the fundamental skills of an activity. But they differ in their assessment of the value and impact of competition in the learning process.

As we've seen, the competitive model believes competition is good virtually from the start of the learning process. The Effortless Learning model sees the premature introduction of competition as a detriment to learning, and asserts that practical, mental and emotional skill development is dramatically enhanced when competition is removed from the process.

My own experience as a learner, a competitor, and a teacher, supports the view of the non-competitive model – that competition works at cross-purposes with learning and attaining excellence. In my experience, the Effortless Learning model significantly increases the percentage of students who achieve excellence, and significantly reduces the less-than-optimal physical, mental and emotional habits produced in students in the competitive system. The focus on learning and mastering practical, mental and emotional skills in a non-competitive environment, virtually guarantees excellence in time.

Phases of Learning and Mastery

The following chart illustrates the crucial difference between competitive and non-competitive education.

Competitive and Non-Competitive Learning Comparison

	Effortless Phase
Competitive Phase	Competitive Phase (Optional)
	Learning Phase
Learning Phase	

TIME >

Conventional Learning   **Effortless Learning**

The chart shows the conventional learning model, with a brief learning phase – which can last as little as a few days – before we begin competing. Once the competitive phase begins, it lasts as long as we play the game. From this point forward, competing and learning go together. In practice, virtually every exercise is geared toward competing; and virtually all of our actions occur in the anticipatory shadow and pressure of competition.

In the Effortless Learning program, there are three phases to the game: the learning phase, an optional competitive phase, and the beyond-competition, or effortless phase. In the learning phase, we learn all the fundamental skills of the game in a non-competitive environment. In tennis or any other high-skill, fine-motor-coordination activity, this phase typically takes a minimum of two years — if we practice a lot — and closer to five years if we practice less frequently. As we see from the chart, the learning phase is significantly longer in the Effortless Learning system than in conventional learning. This is a good thing.

People ask me if there can be a competitive phase of Effortless Learning. The answer is, yes. Developing confidence in and mastery of our skills in a non-competitive environment improves our performance in competition, if we choose to compete. But in the effortless model, competition is a completely optional phase. Some people feel a need to prove themselves to others or to themselves. Some, raised in a competitive system, believe competing is necessary to measure their progress and prove their skills. Some simply enjoy competing. So they can compete if they choose.

And, after going through an optional competitive phase in the Effortless Learning model, it's time to move into the effortless phase, where we hone our skills to the point of mastery without the distractions of competition. Remember, people who compete against us try and do everything in their power to win. And in the dog-eat-dog competitive system, this often includes the unsavory aspects of competition, such as trying to destabilize our self-confidence, conscious or subconscious cheating, and various other forms of poor sportsmanship.

We may play well in competition, but it's impossible to play our absolute best under such conditions. We play and learn better in a healthy and supportive environment where everyone is helping us be our best. Once we have attained true excellence by mastering the basic skills, we may choose to compete again or not. But it will be by our own choice, for our own reasons. Peak performance occurs most reliably in a cooperative environment.

A Developmental Difference of Opinion

Today, many experts in childhood education believe children are developmentally ready to handle competition at around the age of nine or ten, although in practice children are introduced to competition much earlier. These experts assert that children of age nine or ten have reached a stage of psychological development where they can deal with the psychological complexities of competition without being harmed by competition's negative side effects.

I completely disagree. I don't believe that age alone is a determining factor in one's ability to handle competition. To be able to handle competition at any age, *we must have sufficiently developed our basic skills and have healthy self-esteem, or real emotional maturity.* Such children (and perhaps even adults) are rare exceptions.

Many people feel that putting children into a little "friendly" competition when they are young is good for them; it gets them to learn how the real world operates. While premature competition may help them understand the way the world currently works, it will also begin instilling patterns of uncertainty, less-than-optimal mechanics, and performance anxiety into their subconscious – patterns that will affect them in many areas of their lives, most likely for the rest of their lives.

A competitive learning environment produces an inevitable focus on the score, on who's winning and losing. After a contest the first question is never "How'd you play?" but "Who won?" The resulting pressure to perform distracts us from focusing on the fundamental skills. Few (if any) children are developmentally prepared to handle the complex stresses of learning *and* competing simultaneously.

Learning works best in a positive, nurturing, creative environment that encourages students and ignites their desire to learn and excel without placing undue pressure on them to succeed or "win" before they have attained basic proficiency. Psychologists David and Roger Johnson concluded from their research on learning that, "cooperative learning situations, compared with competitive and individualistic situations, promote higher levels of self-esteem and healthier processes for deriving conclusions about one's self-worth." And Alfie Kohn has noted: "A number of psychologists have proposed that optimal human functioning presupposes a sense of security about the world — a confidence that it is a safe place and one's needs will be met."

Effortless Learning, or excellence-based non-competitive education, works better for students of all levels, abilities, and ages. Having worked with many hundreds of students for many years, I can say that beginning adults and children find non-competitive learning easier, less frustrating, more nurturing and enjoyable. Removing the artificial stress of competition from the natural challenges of learning a new skill enables them to learn more deeply, and at their own pace.

Effortless Learning also allows intermediate students to focus more fully on mastering basic skills, and to better handle, and move more quickly through the challenges and frustrations of their level of development. And finally, Effortless Learning allows advanced students the time, opportunity and undivided focus to return to, rediscover and hone fundamentals that may have been missed or inadequately developed while learning in a competitive system. Bottom line, practicing and mastering basic skills in a nurturing environment of collaborative learning with other learners, instead of against rivals doing everything within their power to defeat one another, produces the best skills and attitudes in all participants.

If we can teach students in a non-competitive environment from the beginning of their involvement, not only will they develop faster, be better, go farther, and have more fun, they will also internalize a healthy and effective model for learning the next activity that they want to learn. This is one of the most significant benefits of the Effortless Learning model; it provides a healthy and effective road map or blueprint for learning any activity. Once we understand how the learning process works, we can learn almost anything we desire. Put another way, in a competitive model, we learn in order to compete; in a non-competitive model, we learn how to learn.

Just as Challenging but More Fun

A non-competitive environment removes external pressure to "win," diminishes fears of losing, and allows us to have more fun with the learning process, to appreciate and enjoy each level of development, even when we're not doing as well as we would like. Working on the fundamentals at each level increasingly patterns skills into our cellular memory. Over time our execution of the fundamentals becomes progressively masterful, nuanced and individualized.

Different activities have different degrees of less-than-optimal performance built into their structure. In tennis, players hit hundreds of shots in a short period of time. This involves many little "failures" as our body and reflexes become accustomed to a new and unnatural activity. Effortless Learning allows us to experience less-than-optimal performance as a natural part of the developmental process, rather than as "failure." What we call failure in a competitive model is simply feedback in the effortless model. There is no failure in Effortless Learning, only less than optimal performance. This allows us to truly let go of the concept of failure and the negative and distracting emotions it engenders, and continually move back toward positive emotions. I call this "having fun with failure." As I tell my students, "When you can have fun with failure, imagine how great success will feel." The shame-based "failure" common to the competitive model is far less an inhibiting factor in Effortless Learning.

Removing Fear as a Motivator

Part of the source of this shame inherent in "losing" within a competitive model is the fact that fear is so often used as a motivating force in childrearing and education. Winning, offered as a way to achieve self-esteem, becomes highly motivating in an atmosphere of fear, or even conditional love. Removing competition from the learning process wouldn't in itself ensure that fear wasn't used as a method of motivating students or enforcing discipline. But it would significantly alleviate the tensions common to a competitive learning environment, and initiate a profound shift in our culture. Finding the will and the wisdom to do this is a great challenge.

Fear, used as a primary motivator throughout history, is considered to be essential to the learning process, or perhaps a necessary evil. Parents, teachers, and employers often use some form of fear to motivate apparently stubborn or lazy children or employees.

In earlier times, and in rare cases today, fear was overtly used as a respectable childrearing method. Children were routinely coerced, intimidated, threatened and even beaten into compliance. In *For Your Own Good*, renowned psychologist Alice Miller has thoroughly addressed the historical use and social/cultural consequences of such childrearing practices. Parents and teachers in every era face a great challenge. It can seem easier to motivate with threats of punishment and consequences than to patiently work through issues with children or students.

* If you are interested in this subject, I highly recommend reading Living Joyfully with Children, by my friends Win and Bill

Sweet (see the Recommended Reading and Resources section at the back of this book), who lay out a map to raise children without using fear as a motivator.

Information Retention

One of the most significant benefits of the Effortless Learning model is the quantity and quality of information we are able retain when competition is removed from the learning process. It is a much larger percentage than in a competitive system. The reason is that in Effortless Learning we continually work on improving and mastering the fundamental skills at every level, from beginning, through intermediate, to advanced. And we don't move to our next level until we have mastered the present level. This exclusive focus on learning and mastering each level in turn locks more correct information into our cellular memory.

At first, development proceeds slowly. But years of practice yield an ever-increasing depth of knowledge and skill, with exponential shifting points where all our previous work comes together to propel us to our next level. And what we have learned stays with us because it is so deeply patterned into our cellular memory.

In a competitive environment, we are often thrown in over our heads, and forced to work on many skill levels simultaneously, regardless of our actual proficiency. But attempting to learn advanced skills before we've mastered the basic skills is counter-productive. Chances are, we won't achieve proficiency at either level. Not giving people sufficient time to learn and develop correct physical skills prior to competing also tends to prevent their developing healthy emotional and psychological skills as well.

Developing Rhythm

Another benefit of a non-competitive system is developing a strong sense of rhythm, one of the skills required to be great at anything. There is a rhythm to everything we do. When we first begin an activity we have little rhythm, especially as it pertains to that activity. As our skills and coordination improve, we start finding our rhythm.

It is significantly harder to develop good rhythm in a competitive system. The goal of all good competitors is to do whatever they need to do to keep their opponents "off" or "out of" their rhythm. The last thing we want is our opponent to have good rhythm. If we can break our opponent's rhythm we have a much better chance of winning.

In Effortless Tennis, since our goal is sustaining the rally for as long as possible by working cooperatively with our partners, we are able to develop our own rhythm while learning how to be in rhythm with others. In Effortless Learning, we fall into the natural rhythm of the learning process itself. We also help each other develop our rhythmic skills. This is anathema in a competitive environment, but this is where peak performance will be experienced. The better the other player's rhythm, the better our rhythm. When our own sense of rhythm is strong, it doesn't matter whether we are competing or not. To play to our potential and get into the zone, we need to be in rhythm with ourselves and with one another. When our sense of rhythm is strong, it is easier to stay focused and relaxed when chaos reigns around us.

Reacting Faster as We Age

In a competitive system, as we age it becomes increasingly difficult to keep up with younger competitors, whether in sports or business. More and more people are able to get the better of us, making it less fun to play. In competitive sports, it seems our skills keep diminishing as younger players win. In business, when younger workers start winning, older workers find themselves out of a job.

In a non-competitive system, we continue to improve with age on many skill levels – physical, mental, emotional and even spiritual. And we can compete if we choose. We have a completely different relationship – an effortless relationship – to winning and losing that allows us maximum enjoyment, regardless of any game's outcome. *We don't have to compete to feel good about ourselves.* We can have fun playing, practicing, and working on our skills and fitness. This is where we discover our full potential and the true joy of mastery.

Not only can we continue getting better with age, we can also quicken our reaction time. We have been led to believe that as we age our reaction time inevitably slows down. But this isn't what I've observed. Our bodies may slow down. But we can continue to develop and improve in our awareness, our anticipation, even our reactions.

And we can experience shifts into new levels of mastery that are as rewarding as our previous shifts.

Few of us have really worked on developing our reaction times to their full potential, and there is almost always room for improvement. We can only start to decline after we have developed our skills to our highest level. And there are skill levels to be attained that do not depend on, and even transcend, the physical. Morihei Ueshiba, the founder of the martial art, Aikido, demonstrated this power to perform at the highest levels of a "sport" well beyond the age of retirement. Film footage showing Ueshiba, in his eighties, effortlessly defeating multiple highly trained attackers many decades younger than himself prove my point.

In a non-competitive environment, players' anticipation and reactions continually improve with age since they continue working on the fundamentals and improving their skills. Practicing the fundamentals at each level of mastery enables us to perceive, assess and react more quickly and efficiently because our body is able to access recorded images of thousands of other similar movements from past practice. In any sport, skill or event, the ability to assess a situation more quickly enables us to more quickly come up with an appropriate and effective response.

Many people use the excuse of aging as their reason for not performing well. And they believe it. But it is not an inherent reality. A non-competitive learning model gives us access to our virtually unlimited potential, and allows us to venture as far as our inherent abilities and determination will take us — even as we get older.

Working Through Frustration and Anger

One of the most difficult aspects of learning is getting through the natural frustration that is part of the learning process. In my experience, most people have a relatively high level of physical and emotional tension already patterned into their cellular memory. Tennis and many other sports and activities involves the necessary development of fine motor-coordination in executing specific, often unfamiliar movements. Beginners, at first unable to correctly perform these new movements often experience unpleasant emotions hardwired into their cellular memory. We all seem to want to be great immediately, but being great instantly isn't realistic. We know what to do intellectually, but the information isn't yet part of our cellular memory. If people recognize that this is what is happening when they fail, rather than telling themselves that they aren't good enough, they can then more easily let go of the frustration. Frustration can be a motivator that makes us more determined to succeed, but if we are frustrated while we are engaged in the field of our endeavor, we are not going to do our best.

In a non-competitive environment, it is easier to work through the frustration of learning because our ego and self-esteem aren't as much on the line. Trying to work through frustration in competition is virtually impossible. It is always there just below the surface and will bubble up any time we perform below our expectations. The interesting thing is that when competition is removed and the frustration is still present, we know we are working with an underlying psychological distress that needs to be dealt with before we can excel. This underlying frustration is most likely the result of a combination of not being in a nurturing environment when we were learning, not being taught how to really learn when we were younger, and being prematurely thrust into competition before we knew what we were doing.

As frustration mounts, anger typically rises to the surface. Again, we get angry because we can't do what we think we should be able to do. Most of the time this means that we haven't put enough time into mastering what it is we are getting angry about. It's easy to understand why we get angry in a competitive environment; we are failing where we feel a need to be succeeding. Just as with frustration, in the short term, anger can be a motivator. Unfortunately, in the long term, getting angry only limits how well we will do in the future.

In a competitive system, people have often learned to use frustration and anger as a means of deflecting criticism; if they get frustrated and angry with *themselves*, it is less likely that an authority figure will yell at them when they make mistakes. Children learn this response from having to deal with parents, teachers, or coaches who may be overly critical. Getting angry with themselves is an effective way for children to get these authority figures to leave them alone.

Many times when we experience frustration and anger, we just give up on what we are doing. We quit. But learning to work through these emotions helps us develop our ability to persevere through tough times. In a non-competitive environment, there is no good reason for us to get to the point of anger. We are just working on developing the skills to be good at what we are doing.

We need to get as much of the frustration and anger out of the learning process as possible because these emotions tend to lower performance, but we also need to teach children and adults how to deal with, and work through, frustration and anger. If anger keeps showing up, its appearance gives us an opportunity to examine our lives more carefully and see what the real cause of our anger might be. Usually our anger is coming from another area in our lives that is unrelated to the current situation. It is important to acknowledge our mistakes, but then we need to get on with what we are doing. As I like to say, "If we can't be best friends with ourselves, how can we expect anyone else to give us a break?"

Removing competition from the learning process doesn't make negative emotional patterns disappear instantly. It can take years to ingrain new, healthy patterns into our cellular memory. I've seen this happen in my students countless times over the years. As people see themselves improving, their frustration and anger tend to melt away. It takes time for this to happen since the pattern of becoming frustrated and angry was programmed over the course of many years. Yet as we practice and develop our outer and inner skills, slowly but surely, these patterns will change.

Gentleness

Working through our frustration and anger in a non-competitive environment allows us to be at ease under pressure, fully present and responsive in the midst of action. And, equally important, it teaches us how to be gentle with our self and others. Most of us tend to tense up, panic or lash out when we get nervous or upset with our self or others. Learning gentleness in our chosen activity helps us to develop practical skills, and emotional stability as well.

The Iroquois Indians of North America say, "Gentleness is our greatest strength." But gentleness isn't a quality that is taught or encouraged in the competitive system, which equates being gentle with being weak or wimpy. The belief is that we can't be tough and gentle simultaneously, that these are mutually exclusive qualities. Yet perhaps this isn't true. Tibetan Buddhism speaks of "ruthless compassion," or exercising power with a gentle spirit, as an aspect of enlightened consciousness. When someone is trying to kick our butt, gentleness isn't a normal reaction. Yet to evolve to a more advanced consciousness requires the ability to be gentle as well as strong.

Gentleness is an essential human quality, and essential to the learning process. I teach gentleness in my Effortless Tennis program by having players learn to hit the ball gently. We must be able to hit the ball gently with efficient mechanics before we can control it and hit it powerfully. Learning to hit the ball gently is an excellent meditative practice. To play gently both requires and develops the skills of relaxation, concentration, fine motor coordination, patience, and more. At first it is extremely difficult to play gently because we haven't developed all of the above qualities relative to a new activity. But practicing "gentle strokes" in sports or in life significantly improves all our skill sets over time. And these gentle habits enhance our power, and become part of our cellular memory.

Physical Health

Non-competitive learning has positive health benefits. Not rushing into competition allows us to develop the fundamentals thoroughly, in a relatively stress-free environment, making injuries less likely. In tennis and other sports, it is easier for players to ingrain efficient techniques, and avoid incorrect stress-induced habits that tend to cause injury. Improper technique is a leading cause of sports injuries.

We are often told in competitive events to "give 110 percent", but it's impossible to give more than 100 percent! By trying to give more we are often working too hard, and over-exerting. This can cause injuries, and even death. We've all heard stories of athletes, from high school competitors to top professionals, collapsing and dying during practice from over-exertion. This 110 percent "no pain, no gain" mentality is pervasive in competitive sports and results in countless injuries and some deaths each year. In a non-competitive system, we get a great workout that is pleasurable and keeps us in good physical shape, without having to hurt ourselves.

The same 110 percent principle holds true in many high-stress, competitive professions, from academics to business to politics. Burning the candle at both ends can lead to minor, acute and even chronic illnesses. But if we apply the principles of Effortless Learning, we can master the fundamentals and achieve mental and emotional maturity without damaging our health. We can function at our peak while maintaining good physical and mental health that allows us to perform in our field of endeavor for the long term.

Psychological Health

After seeing how a non-competitive education system improves learning and performance and reduces stress, it is logical to conclude that it would benefit our long-term psychological health. If we are learning and performing better in a more positive and healthy environment, and getting closer to achieving our potential, it only follows that our self-esteem and overall psychological health will be better too.

The competitive system, in contrast, with its built-in pressures, its unbalanced focus on winning, on fear of losing, on external rewards, and all of the resulting unhealthy side-effects discussed in these pages, works against overall psychological health. Many destabilizing effects occur on a subconscious level activated by negative patterns etched into our cellular memory.

Perhaps the biggest benefit to psychological health from a non-competitive system is the sense of inner accomplishment and corresponding self-esteem gained by years of training and the development of excellence in our chosen field. We reap similar psychological benefits as we see ourselves growing and transcending old emotional and psychological baggage around winning and losing. This experience of developing maturity, of self-control and self-mastery on emotional and psychological levels, is profoundly rewarding, and a significant source of self-esteem.

Effortless Learning offers a diametric opposite to the adversarial and externally focused competitive model. It offers an inner-values focused model of healthy partnership and mutual support in practical and emotional skill building. Non-competitive learning strengthens our sense of self-worth and our ability to trust and work fruitfully with others. It provides more real camaraderie with less negativity than the competitive model. The Effortless Learning model removes stress by removing competition from the learning process, and begins to undo psychological damage caused by experiences of premature or unhealthy competition.

The Thrill of Accomplishment

An unrecognized and unappreciated aspect of non-competitive learning, from a competitive perspective, is that non-competitive learning develops all the perceived benefits touted in the competitive model. Exercise, excitement, camaraderie, teamwork, challenging ourselves and developing to the fullest of our abilities, learning "winning strategies" and more can all be experienced without competition. The only element of competition not realized in a non-competitive environment is the thrill of victory — the big element that seems to capture everyone's attention. We love to feel the rush of victory!

The reality is that one person's "thrill of victory" is another person's "agony of defeat". For every winner, there is a loser. In a non-competitive learning system, the thrill of victory is replaced by the more satisfying and intrinsic thrill of accomplishment, and also the joy of true camaraderie. This multi-leveled process that competition obstructs and obscures is supported, revealed and fully realized through non-competitive learning. The thrill of accomplishment and the joy of true camaraderie are more profound and healing experiences than the thrill of victory. Their fruits, greater than external trophies and public recognition, are the inner rewards of emotional and spiritual growth.

The Importance of Competent Teaching

In my non-competitive tennis program, I teach all the skills required to be a *great* tennis player — without any competition in the process. The short-term goals are learning and skill building. The long-term goals are excellence, or mastery of the skills of the game, and self-mastery in the game of life. These goals can be fully attained without competing. But it requires competent teachers who understand the principles and the process of non-competitive learning.

This matter of competent teachers is key. Unfortunately, in our current competitive learning system there are many teachers who are not fully competent. Because the competitive learning model promotes teaching the "next" level before proficiency has been attained, most teachers are unable to help many of their students master the basic skills. And many teachers, products of the competitive learning model, have themselves not achieved mastery of practical skills or genuine human maturity. Ill-prepared and inadequate teachers misinform far too many students. Most of us had such teachers in school. (The athletic coach assigned to teach history is a common example.) As a result, many teachers are unqualified "professionals" passing on the flaws of the competitive model, along with inadequate information and skills in their subjects, to the next generation.

Non-competitive Teaching

In some ways, teaching is easier in a non-competitive educational system; in other ways it is much more challenging. Teaching is easier in a non-competitive system because there is far more repetition of material. This makes it easier for teachers and students to learn to the point of mastering fundamentals. Students aren't rushed along the learning process at an arbitrary pace, so teachers are able to work with students at their own individual pace. The necessary time for learning is allowed in an environment that encourages learning and proficiency over winning and "passing".

A competitive system weeds out those who "can't keep up", and hides the prevalence of insufficient learning with "passing" grades from A to D, or a learning percentage of 100% to 60%. This arbitrary system allows us all to avoid facing the fact that most students "pass" without really learning much of their subjects.

Teaching is more challenging in a non-competitive system because teachers are responsible for their students actually learning, rather than merely passing. In this more rigorous and repetitive learning environment, teachers must be fully knowledgeable in their subjects, and be more focused, persistent and patient. They must create a nurturing, supportive, structured environment in which learning can take place. They must be able to lead students through each phase of learning, from beginning to final mastery. And they must stay committed to their students throughout the journey. It is much easier to let students "pass" with partial comprehension, than work with them in a rigorous and systematic way until they achieve full comprehension. Part of the problem is that we give teachers too many students to work with, don't pay them sufficiently or allow them the time and means to truly teach our children in this way. Students must also do their part by putting in the time to practice the material.

Yet if teaching is more challenging in a non-competitive environment, the rewards are also greater, not only for individual students who achieve competence and eventually, excellence, but also for the teachers who see their students blossom, as well as for the culture to which these students will contribute.

Possible Drawbacks of Non-competitive Learning

We've covered the positive aspects of non-competitive learning, but are there any drawbacks to the non-competitive model? I've only noticed a few potential drawbacks, mostly arising from the potential clash between the non-competitive model and the current entrenched and dominant competitive model and mindset. But I believe that if the non-competitive learning model became the dominant model, these potential drawbacks might well disappear. These possible drawbacks are:

1: Lack of an External Reward

One of the big draws of competitive learning is the glory and prestige of being a winner. People are motivated by the potential rewards or punishments of the system. Introducing competition prematurely into the learning process makes these external incentives a factor almost from the beginning. But these "bribes" are conspicuously absent in a non-competitive learning environment. This might result in a lack of motivation for those raised in a competitive mindset, for those who believe they are inherently competitive, or for those who have been conditioned to require external rewards for their motivation. (Actually, there is a non-physical form of external reward in the non-competitive system, praise, which is given in acknowledgment of a student's patience, perseverance, self-motivation, accountability, and job well done.) The good news is that since there is no external reward, there is also no punishment. Since more people lose than win in a competitive environment, this makes it easier to accept the lack of external rewards.

Love of an activity for its own sake, and the natural satisfactions of learning and developing new levels of skill, will always be sufficient motivation for some. But achieving excellence takes a great deal of physical, mental, and emotional work and dedication. And since the competitive system uses external rewards and punishments as a main source of motivation, some will find it difficult to self-motivate for the love of the activity. Over the course of time, however, as people are weaned off the need for an external reward, self-motivation will blossom.

2: Lack of Patience and the Will to Persevere

A second possible drawback to non-competitive learning is its inherently long-term nature. Our modern American culture discourages delayed gratification. As a result, many people have a hard time persisting over the long-term and learning at higher levels to the point of mastery. We want to be good *now*, and if that doesn't happen we may get bored and decide to try something else. Almost everyone responds positively to his or her early experiences with Effortless Tennis. But comprehensive learning of anything is always challenging, mentally, emotionally, and, depending on the activity, physically.

The competitive model provides a short term "thrill" of competition and adrenalin rush. No matter that this interferes with the learning process in the ways I've described here; the fact is that it does offer a compelling distraction from the periodic tedium of in-depth learning.

Any activity that demands long-term commitment to get to the place where it feels *effortless* makes it challenging for people to stay committed. But many people do derive great satisfaction from learning a chosen skill to the point of mastery. There are notable successful areas of non-competitive learning: artists, artisans, scholars, scientists and more have always pursued their chosen fields outside of the competitive model, for love of their chosen activity.

3: Dealing with Uncomfortable Feelings

The third potential drawback to non-competitive learning is that the "excitement" of competition distracts us from uncomfortable feelings lurking beneath the surface of our awareness, feelings most of us prefer to avoid. With the distraction of competition removed from the Effortless Learning process, students often become acutely aware of boredom, restlessness, anxiety, self-doubt, fear of failure or success, and a host of other uncomfortable feelings and emotions.

Most people are reluctant to feel, deal with, or even acknowledge these feelings. This is why people generally prefer "excitement" over learning. The confrontation with these uncomfortable feelings and emotions in the learning process is one of the biggest reasons that people quit before attaining proficiency in many demanding activities.

4: Lack of Societal Support for Non-Competition, and Attachment to Competition

A fourth potential drawback is the current lack of understanding and support for, and even impatience with and mistrust of, a non-competitive model within the larger culture. This is connected to a conditioned and perhaps ingrained attachment to competition. As a result, there are few places to practice non-competitive learning in current society. One of the first things I observed after removing competition from my teaching program is that many people resist the very idea of its elimination. When I first started talking to people about a cooperative approach to learning, many — especially the men — became protective/defensive, as if I were attacking something sacred, almost the way parents might respond to someone threatening their children.

For example, when my tennis students play with people outside of my program, the other players generally want to start competing right away, and tend to become impatient with practice that focuses exclusively on skill development — even when they clearly need such practice. And most teachers automatically include competition as part of the learning process, even early on, and consider the idea of eliminating competition too radical, even while admitting that students can't perform well if they haven't mastered the fundamentals, and that most students are no where close to mastering the fundamentals.

The Bottom Line — For "Competitive" People

Despite these potential drawbacks, my experience, and that of my students, tells me that non-competitive learning is the most effective, healthy and beneficial way to learn. Of course, competitive people always want to know if a non-competitive model will help them to beat somebody else. "Sure, this all sounds good, but will it give me a competitive advantage?"

The answer to their question is an unequivocal yes! A non-competitive learning system isn't geared toward competition, so it may take longer to develop the skills to consistently succeed in the competitive system. But once we get to that level, it is much easier to stay there because our skills, inner and outer, are more well-rounded, deeply-ingrained, and multi-faceted. Many tennis players have used the Effortless Learning approach to develop their games so that they could do well in competition, and it works. One such example is Tarrin, the player I mentioned earlier.

In October 1991 a single mother brought her nine-year-old daughter, Tarrin, to me for tennis lessons. Tarrin's father was a tennis player, so she had some early experience with hand-eye coordination, and it showed. I could see from the first moments on court that this girl was very coordinated, even a "natural". She took lessons for two years until other sports, and life, distracted her.

Tarrin and I reconnected in January 1996, when she was in the eighth grade. We began an intensive program for the next four years, with lessons twice a week, more than forty weeks per year. All of this time we worked within the non-competitive system; we never played any kind of competitive games. I worked with her on developing the skills she needed to be a great player without any competition.

Tarrin started playing competitive tennis on her high-school team in grade nine. In her four years of high school, at the number-one position on her team, she won 90 percent of her matches. She also won the county championship her sophomore and junior years. She would have won three years in a row, but classic adolescent tendencies distracted her focus in her senior year. She still won 83 percent of her matches that year. Tarrin took time off from tennis beginning in the late fall of 1999, and graduated from high school in 2000.

In March 2001, Tarrin returned to the Effortless Tennis program after an absence of nearly a year and a half. Her enthusiasm for the game was back, and we took up right where she left off. We started working together for an hour and a half each week. She enrolled in a nearby community college and joined the tennis team. She was undefeated in the number-one singles position during the regular season. In the Northern California Junior College Championship, she lost in the singles tournament finals to the only other player who was also undefeated for the season. She won the doubles title with her partner, and led her team to the Northern California championship. In the California State Championships for Junior Colleges, she won the doubles title and lost in the semifinals of the singles. These are great results, but the bottom line is that she had managed to ingrain many of the physical, mental, and emotional fundamentals that led to her success before she started competing.

Tarrin, was ranked # 2 in the Women's Open Level (the highest level in amateur tennis) in Northern California in 2004, #1 in 2005, and #3 in 2006, and is now playing some entry-level pro tournaments. Her story shows that non-competitive learning works even for people who want to compete and win. I believe Tarrin's skill would have developed further and more rapidly had competition not been introduced into her learning process in high school. But joining her high school tennis team was a natural progression in the current competitive paradigm, and obviously she did extremely well. No doubt, her years of non-competitive learning were a factor in her success. And, had she started her non-competitive training in early childhood, I believe she might have developed the skill to be a top tennis professional.

The Future of Sports

I believe a non-competitive learning model will improve performance in sports whether competing is involved or not. Higher levels of excellence – physical, mental and emotional – will make learning, playing and watching more exciting than ever. There will still be a time and place for competition, but competition won't be the inhibiting factor in the learning process that it is now.

A non-competitive learning model will encourage many more people to participate in, learn and become truly competent in a wider range of activities. It will also allow people to enjoy learning and practicing the basic skills with supportive non-competitive partners, and to experience the deeper mutual thrill of attaining excellence, and helping others to do the same. It will encourage more people to become physically fit. The Effortless Learning model will allow people to perform consistently at a high level over the long term, even into old age.

I also believe that the emotional balance and maturity that the non-competitive model promotes will have a positive impact on professional sports, and allow athletics to more fully achieve and demonstrate our human potential. There will be amazing contests, with little or no psychological and physical negativity. Individuals and teams will play closer to their potential on a more consistent basis. Spectators will be on the edge of their seats, riveted to the highest levels of performance, and instructed by the display of civility and fair play between individual opponents and opposing teams. Poor sportsmanship in general, and the random savagery we see exhibited in some sports, will largely disappear. As will the occasional violence we see on the part of spectators, which the competitive model unconsciously encourages in various ways.

No matter what the field of endeavor, non-competitive learning will maximize the positives and diminish the negatives. Working cooperatively and pooling our ideas will yield more satisfying and productive results at every level. Businesses and government will run more efficiently. Products will continue to improve, making our lives better.

But the biggest benefits will be cultural, as the non-competitive model will call out and develop the best in everyone. We will enable our children to learn and grow to their fullest potential. Over time, generations of children learning in a non-competitive environment will yield unparalleled advances in all areas of learning. Effortless Learning will open up new dimensions of human skill and development, of human relations, and human evolution in general.

I believe that these benefits, which are the ultimate goals of Effortless Learning, only scratch the surface of what is possible. And they are attainable.

PART THREE
Effortless Learning

Believe it if you need it
Or leave it if you dare
— Robert Hunter

5
Fundamentals of Learning

If we advance confidently in the direction of our dreams,
and endeavor to live the life which we have imagined,
we will meet with a success unexpected in common hours.
— Henry David Thoreau

To learn anything to the level of excellence, we must learn *how* to learn. It sounds simple, but the reality is that many of us don't know how to learn. This ignorance makes the learning process more difficult and less enjoyable than it could be. Understanding the fundamentals of non-competitive learning enhances our learning process in any field. It makes the journey easier and more enjoyable. When we understand how we learn, we know what to do to increase our skill at each level. We are also less disturbed by the seeming ups and downs, recognizing them as natural phases in a long-term process that leads to increasing mastery. Once we grasp the fundamentals of non-competitive learning, we can learn anything so long as we are willing to practice and persevere for the years that it takes to attain mastery.

In this chapter I present eight fundamentals of learning:

1. Core Information
2. The Sequential Nature of Learning
3. Conscious/Subconscious Learning
4. Slow-Motion Learning
5. The Principle of "Less Than Optimal"
6. Everything We Know Is Wrong
7. Learning Plateaus
8. Mental-Lightness Training

1. CORE INFORMATION

To build a skyscraper you must first build a strong foundation. The same is true for excellence. Attaining excellence in any subject requires mastering the core information, the basics or fundamentals, of that subject. Every subject or skill is comprised of its core information, and learning all of it is mandatory. We can't pick and choose parts of this information that we like, avoid other parts we don't find interesting, and still learn effectively. It doesn't matter how gifted we may be. To attain proficiency, achieve mastery, or fulfill our potential in any endeavor, all of the core information must be imprinted in our cellular memory.

Core information has two parts: the universal and the specific. Ideally, both are learned simultaneously. The skills we develop by mastering universal core information give us a foundation in what I call the *Keys to Peak Performance*. These universal skills or keys are: joy, relaxation, concentration, patience, perseverance, self-motivation, accountability, fitness, coordination, and efficient skill development. They facilitate and accelerate the learning process in any field. They also facilitate our overall human growth and development in all areas of life. That's why they are universal. I will describe these keys in more detail in the next chapter.

The second part of core information, the specific, differs in any particular field and is unique to each activity. There is core information for being an accountant, an architect, a teacher, a scuba diver, a UPS driver, a chef, and so on. To excel in any occupation we must learn and master its distinctive basics. The learning process itself is relatively simple; we work on or practice this core information, mastering each level, from the basics to the most advanced, in a natural progression.

2. THE SEQUENTIAL NATURE OF LEARNING

The second fundamental of learning is this: *there is a necessary sequence to anything we want to learn.* Step A leads to Step B which leads to Step C, and so on. Skipping steps is always problematic, and always complicates the learning process. We don't leap from Step A to Step E just because Step E seems more interesting or fun. But skipping steps for superficial reasons of ego or gratification is common in our hurry-up society and natural in the competitive learning system. We want it now. We want to be better than we are, further ahead than we are. We want to be winners right away rather than students diligently practicing essential skills until they are etched in our cellular memory. We're afraid that if we don't move forward we will be left behind.

Most students in most subjects move ahead to more advanced materials or levels before they master the basics. And most people don't like to admit they're not as good as they wish they were or believe they are, and return to an earlier phase of learning. The ego, a big obstacle to learning, balks at the obvious: if we're not proficient at our present level, the intelligent thing is to return to the previous level, practice there to the point of proficiency, and *then* move ahead.

In reality, if we don't master the basics we *will* be left behind. Skipping steps slows our progress and leaves crucial gaps in our understanding of the basics. This limits our development and our enjoyment, and creates chronic frustration. So in Effortless Learning, we take the time to proceed sequentially.

In tennis, for example, the first thing we learn is the "ready position". This is the stance we take every time we are waiting to hit the ball. If we don't return to the ready position between shots, we won't be fully prepared for the next shot. This is the first physical step players need to ingrain into their cellular memory.

In learning anything, the developmental sequence is more or less the same. More complex skills are built on mastery of the basics. Complex skills and challenges are only pursued after the basics, or previous levels, have been mastered in a less-challenging format. Once we master a series of steps, we start over again with Step A, and take each step to another level. We see this even in professional sports. There's a classic scene in sports movies about this: the team is in a slump, they lose again, the coach shakes his head in disgust and announces that it's time to go back to the drawing board, to return to the basics.

In real life, when a pro team comes out of a slump, interviewers will often ask what turned things around. And the coach or player being interviewed will usually say the same thing: They went back and worked on the fundamentals. The very highest skill levels rest on and emerge from this mastery of the basics. Following the correct sequence, forwards and backwards, is a principle that unfailingly yields rewards when applied, and consequences when violated. Step A leads to Step B leads to Step C. Patience, practice and perseverance are always rewarded.

The following diagram is a playful visual approximation of how learning works.

A>A>A>A>A>A>A>A>A>A>A>A>A>A>A>A>A>A>A>A>B>

A>B>A>B>A>B>A>B>A>B>A>B>A>B>A>B>A>B>A>B>C>

A>B>C>A>B>C>A>B>C>A>B>C>A>B>C>A>B>C>D>

A>B>C>D>A>B>C>D>A>B>C>D>A>B>C>D>A>B>C>D>E>

A>B>C>D>E>A>B>C>D>E>A>B>C>D>E>A>B>C>D>E>F>

A>B>C>D>E>F>A>B>C>D>E>F>A>B>C>D>E>F>G>

A>B>C>D>E>F>G>A>B>C>D>E>F>G>A>B>C>D>E>F>G>H>

As you see above, we practice Step A until we are ready to learn Step B. And even while learning Step B, we are still practicing the Step A skills. If at any point in Step B we run into difficulties, we don't push forward to Step C. We revisit Step A, practice until proficient, then return to Step B, and practice until proficient. This prepares us to move, realistically, to Step C. We repeat this forward/backward/forward process at every level and are never too advanced to return to, and learn from the basics. Thus we master the fundamental skills and build a solid foundation for our skyscraper.

Excelling requires doing an activity in this way, over and over, for years. This is true whether you're a musician, dancer, athlete, physicist, baker, surgeon, writer or computer programmer. Unfortunately, our high-speed culture fosters short attention spans that make it hard for people to enjoy prolonged focused repetition of basic skills. Many people find it "boring".

Boredom is a name we give to the frustration of not being able to perform an activity successfully, or of hitting the limits of our attention span. Either way it is important to work through boredom, develop our skills and our attention span, and come out on the other side. This is the process that leads to both skill development and human maturity. Once we get past this initial learning hump, repetition and the progress it allows, becomes deeply satisfying, even fun. And the enjoyment deepens over time. I say this as someone who has been performing the same activity on a daily basis for over thirty years. Teaching children this way from the start develops their functional skills and their attention span, increases their enjoyment, and diminishes the "boredom" factor.

3. Conscious/Subconscious Learning

Ideally, in learning an academic subject, we read some material, ponder the information, and digest it. Then we move on to the next batch of information and repeat the process. Information we absorb consciously in this fashion eventually becomes part of our subconscious. We access it automatically without having to think about it.

The learning process for a physical skill works a bit differently. We must consciously learn various elements of a functional activity while performing the activity itself. Thus we are engaging two learning processes simultaneously. We must consciously learn and practice the information and the actions until both become part of our subconscious.

I hear two common complaints in my Effortless Tennis program. 1. There is too much to think about while trying to run after and hit the ball. 2. Thinking about the information while trying to perform the activity increases the chances of making mistakes. Both are true. And, both are unavoidable aspects of the learning process. There is no other way to learn, and no learning without a learning curve. Learning is always a conscious process before it becomes an innate or subconscious ability. The initial conscious phase is always challenging. And when the subconscious abilities appear, we know the information and the actions have become ingrained in our cellular memory.

By breaking a skill down to its component parts, it is easier to see how it all fits together, and to then eventually get it all to fit together optimally. It takes time to go through this process, and if we are immediately put into competition, we won't have the time to develop these sub-skills. Before we can hope to perform an action without thinking about it, we have to know each component part. First we are conscious of everything that we are doing and need to do, and then as we rehearse it, it becomes part of our subconscious, stored in our cellular memory.

For some time, this approach is challenging, but the results will bear out. Some teachers feel that learning in this manner takes away from a player's spontaneity, but in the long run, I have seen that this approach gives players much more freedom to express themselves and play to their potential. A prime example of this is learning the scales in music. Once the mechanics of the different scales are part of the cellular memory, spontaneity naturally appears and flourishes. Eventually, everything happens without conscious effort. When we reach this point, we have the greatest opportunity for spontaneity. Our performance and our game finally feel effortless.

4. SLOW-MOTION LEARNING

Our mind and body can integrate more information, more thoroughly, when we slow down the learning process. The competitive system tries to accelerate the learning process by giving more information than we can comprehend and assimilate in a given time frame. The artificial "solution" to this dilemma is memorization, which is not the same as comprehension. Comprehension etches information into our cellular memory. Memorization without comprehension does not.

In a competitive learning environment where we often have to keep up or fall behind, memorization becomes a default strategy for "success", which means passing tests. And passing tests becomes a default substitute for actually learning and mastering the material. Memorization without comprehension enables us to temporarily retain more information than we can comprehend and digest in a short period of time, in order to pass tests. This gives the appearance of learning and comprehension, and the outer rewards that go with it. It is a natural choice in an unreal and counterproductive competitive environment, especially since the alternative is failure or being labeled a slow learner. Next to being labeled a loser, there is no worse epithet in our culture than being labeled a slow learner.

Effortless Learning knows that slow learning fosters deeper comprehension that becomes true knowledge, which makes long-term memorization possible. For this reason, slow learning is essential for true comprehension and mastery in any field.

Slow-motion learning is also essential to the mastery of any physical skill. Slower movement allows a kind of micro-awareness that etches patterns and information more deeply into our cellular memory. A common and effective learning method in music is to learn to play a piece at a much slower tempo. Once we can perform the piece slowly, we gradually speed it up until we can play it at its proper tempo. In this process, all of the elements required to play the piece are deeply etched into our cellular memory. This same scenario can be applied to sports or any other physical activity.

Slow learning allows us to experience, absorb and anchor in our body/mind more of the physical and emotional feelings, as well as the techniques, that allow us to play in the zone. When we access these feelings in slow motion, we increase the likelihood of being able to reproduce them at full speed.

5. The Principle of "Less than Optimal"

The fifth fundamental of learning involves a shift in perspective that allows us to view our experiences in a new way. I call this the shift from "bad" to "less-than-optimal". We tend to define experiences we don't like as *bad*, a word with a lot of baggage attached to it. We say we were bad, the shot was bad, the note was bad, the performance was bad, the results of the test were bad, and so on.

This perspective is limited, counterproductive, and distorted. Murder, torture and slavery are bad. Making mistakes in a learning process is not. Mistakes are a natural, unavoidable and instructive part of any learning process. This is a healthy perspective that takes needless shame, guilt and judgment out of the learning process. It frees us up to be more aware, present, focused and creative. It allows our mistakes and our "less-than-optimal" performances to motivate us and show us where we can improve our skills. It also allows us to appreciate, even in our less than optimal moments, the things we did well.

Whether in sports, business, education, or life, our long-term goal is to have as many optimal experiences as possible. But until we have mastered all aspects of our chosen field, we will have many less-than-optimal moments. That's just the way it is.

Changing our wording is more than semantics. It helps change our inner experience of our outer experience. It is crucial to make this shift in our thinking. It's important for the little things we do, but is especially important when we are performing a high-skill activity. It takes time to change our thinking, but seeing something as *less than optimal* instead of *bad* will "unlimit" our potential. The thinking behind these words comes from a deep part of our subconscious. Every time you hear yourself judging something – a shot, an action, a result – as "bad," see if you can switch that thought to "less-than-optimal."

Sometimes we do something that feels *really* off. In Effortless Learning, when we recognize that something we did was far from what we wanted, we announce that it was "way-less-than-optimal." Using the expression "way-less-than-optimal" acknowledges reality with humor, rather than judgment and self-blame. This shift in perspective makes learning more fun, and the bottom line is that it works well.

6. EVERYTHING WE KNOW IS WRONG

Bruce Lipton, the cellular biologist whose work I highlighted earlier, calls this next fundamental of learning *universe humor*. I call it *everything we know is wrong*: We hold certain beliefs that we feel are undeniably true; we have seen these beliefs validated many times before — or so we thought. We would have bet our lives on the validity of certain beliefs. Then we find new information that incontrovertibly contradicts them. Hence, "Everything we know is wrong." Recognizing that what we "knew" to be true, isn't, that we didn't know what we were talking about, can make us confused, angry, and disillusioned. It can lead to self-doubt or denial. Or, it can amuse us, free us up, and open us to new and better ways of thinking, perceiving and acting.

Dr. Lipton was among those biologists who "knew" that our genes determined our behavior. But when he saw the results of the Human Genome Project, he realized that we have far too few genes to do the job, and that we had to *learn* more of our behaviors than he had ever considered possible. Dr. Lipton's response was to laugh at the perverse nature of universe humor.

"Everything we know is wrong" teaches that as the world is vast, constantly changing and evolving, and we are small and limited in our development and perspective, our worldview needs to change and evolve for us to grow into our potential. Buddhists call this approach *beginner's mind.* If we can see with a beginner's mind, with fresh eyes, we are less likely to get stuck in our thinking and development. This is an important fundamental of learning. Encountering new information or truth often challenges our old assumptions. We can either ignore or deny the new and defend the old; or we can open to new information and allow it to expand our awareness and alter our view of reality.

People often cling to old beliefs, fearing what change may bring. But the universe is always nudging us forward as if it doesn't want us to stay stuck. If we don't or won't learn from the nudges – the easy lessons – harder knocks come along to shake our old, obsolete foundation. New information, and the perspective shifts it facilitates, are often the solution to our dilemma, like a light leading us forward to greater awareness, development and mastery of one kind or another.

There are moments in life when we are presented with irrefutable information that contradicts our cherished beliefs and threatens the stability we found in them for a time. These moments are essential to learning, growing and attaining our full potential, because they help us break through old limitations, expand our knowledge and our horizons, and begin to function in new and better ways.

It's hard to admit that a fundamental or cherished belief we have held is wrong. Our egos tend to get in the way of admitting this realization. But as we survive and grow through these experiences, we become less threatened by, and more willing to make necessary adjustments in our thinking and our view of reality. We learn to keep an open mind.

My hope is that the new information about competitive

and non-competitive learning presented in this book will shift your perspective and shake your deeply ingrained belief in the competitive model that is creating more problems than benefits for a vast majority of people. My conviction, based on years of study, exploration and experience, is that in this particular area, *everything we have known is wrong.*

7. LEARNING PLATEAUS

If every teacher and student understood the importance of learning plateaus to the learning process, we would be able to learn anything we desire. Recognizing that all of us learn in a series of plateaus allows each of us to learn at our own pace.

We all have different, even idiosyncratic learning modes or styles. We may learn best verbally, visually, kinesthetically, or in some other fashion, but we all learn in a series of plateaus. One of the difficult truths of the learning process is that we do not constantly improve. There are always times when improvement levels off.

At first, learning any new subject is challenging. Then at some point we may see sudden and rapid improvement. I've found that beginning tennis players seem to learn quickly in the first six months. Then they tend to hit a learning plateau where they don't seem to improve as quickly, or even seem to fall back or get worse. After a while, they often have a breakthrough and the cycle starts again as they shift to their next level. The learning process is often three steps forward, one or two steps back, and three steps forward again, with regular time spent on plateaus. This is especially true with high-skill activities.

The more we improve, the greater the challenges of the next level. If we stay with an activity through the first plateau, we typically experience the next leap in improvement somewhere around the one-year mark. People who don't persevere and practice through their first year of learning a new skill, don't get to experience this leap. There is of course a direct correlation between how much we practice and how quickly we develop our skills and move through the plateaus. Some people will reach this next plateau in ten months, for others it may be fourteen months.

Most of our improvement is a matter of how much we practice and length of time we are involved with an activity. In that sense, the learning process is a simple equation: The more we practice, the longer we persevere, the better we get. And there are plateaus all along the way. The process of learning, absorbing and integrating new information can be effectively streamlined, but it can't be rushed. No matter how much we practice, it will still take a certain length of time to excel. Information and skills are ingrained into our cellular memory more deeply over time. Learning is cumulative.

After the first-year leap, it typically takes another year of diligent study and practice before we experience the next-level shift of integration and improvement, and the next plateau. This second-year learning plateau typically lasts anywhere from one to three years. That means the next shift into a higher level of skill and knowledge will occur somewhere between the three to five year mark.

The more advanced we get, the longer the plateaus and the smaller the increments of improvement. We don't continually make the same leaps in improvement that we did in earlier phases. But the plateaus are so much higher and so much more enjoyable as we approach and attain mastery. If we have persisted with the same commitment and diligence through the five-year mark, we will feel confident in our skills, they will be indelibly etched into our cellular memory, and we will be able to enjoy the activity at a high level for the rest of our lives.

With consistent and diligent practice, an initial level of mastery can be achieved around the ten-year mark. After the five-year mark, the learning plateaus in high-skill fields generally occur in about five-year increments, even after mastery is attained. We are still improving during these plateaus, but these improvements are subtle and often imperceptible. Until we shift to a next level. If we persist in our pursuit of excellence, our development will continue after twenty years, after thirty years, and more. Every activity has its own learning plateaus of different durations, and to grow, we are required to move along them.

Following is a chart that applies to high-skill activities.

Learning Plateaus Chart

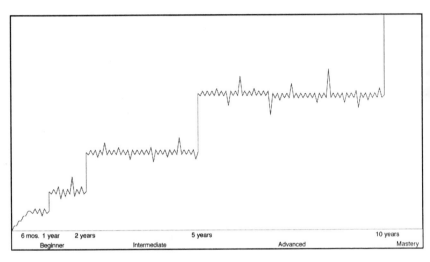

6 mos. 1 year	2 years		5 years		10 years
Beginner		Intermediate		Advanced	Mastery

Individual times will vary depending on quantity and quality of practice.

The premature emphasis on competition doesn't allow us to pass through these natural learning progressions. From our competitive culture, we expect that we have to win *now*! Winning isn't something that we wait around to accomplish for two to five years — that seems like a lifetime. Our competitive system has led us to believe that winning is supposed to occur in the near future — if not sooner. But if we don't have the skills, the wins will be few and far between, the frustration will be great, and the learning process will be significantly restricted.

In a competitive system countless people are weeded out before they have a chance to work through these natural learning plateaus. Remember the high-school player I mentioned earlier, John, who went from non-athlete to athlete? It took him three years to develop enough skill to be successful in competition. Without a non-competitive approach, John would have been another victim of the system. There are millions of people like John who were never given the chance to get their skills together. These learning plateaus mark the big-picture steps of mastery. We need to make them an integral part of the learning process.

8. MENTAL LIGHTNESS TRAINING

The last fundamental of learning involves our emotional/ psychological condition. The big catch phrase for the past twenty years in sports psychology has been *mental toughness.* Sports psychologist Dr. Jim Loehr was already talking about mental toughness back in 1983, when I took a weeklong workshop with him. His mental-toughness training program for tennis was the first of its kind.

The idea that we have to be mentally tough to deal with pressure and overcome adversity goes back further than Sparta in ancient Greece. Developing mental toughness decreases the likelihood of our breaking down in pressure-packed moments. Dr. Loehr listed seven components of mental toughness, all of which can be developed. They are: self-confidence, arousal control, attention control, visual and imagery control, motivational control, positive energy, and attitude control. These elements served as some of the prototypes for the Keys to Peak Performance that I will be describing in the next chapter.

Yet the idea of mental toughness, of "being tough", is philosophically and energetically tied to the competitive model. It tells us we have to be tough, project toughness, be perceived as tough, or we will be defeated. Such thinking is common in sports, business, politics, and more. In some environments and cultures, it is an essential aspect of daily life. The majority of our movie heroes, from Humphrey Bogart, Gary Cooper and John Wayne, to Sylvester Stallone, Arnold Schwarzenegger and Bruce Willis, embody this model.

Mental *strength,* possessing mental clarity, focus and stamina, is a good thing. But this is different than the attitude of mental toughness commonly promoted, which can make us rigid, inflexible and overly aggressive. Trying to be tough can make our minds and muscles constrict, slowing our thinking and inhibiting our movements. The idea of "toughness" is linked to, and often a reaction or compensatory response to a deep-seated fear of losing. To the degree that this is so, it is really a subliminal meditation on fear.

Mental lightness is different than mental toughness. It is in fact its complementary spiritual opposite. It is essential to the learning process, and to attaining mastery and peak performance. Mental lightness allows us to be relaxed, present and aware under great pressure or in the midst of intense action. It also enables us to absorb more information in a shorter time with less effort than when we are in serious/intense mode.

Three great examples of mental lightness in our era were Mahatma Ghandi, Morihei Ueshiba, founder of Aikido, and Muhammed Ali. Mental lightness enabled Ghandi to face setbacks, adversity and even imprisonment, with an imperturbable calmness. It allowed him to defeat the British Empire without firing a shot or resorting to willful opposition, anger, enmity or any other qualities common to a competitive model. Mental lightness enabled Ueshiba to defeat multiple opponents while remaining in a state of physical and mental relaxation, heightened awareness, and visible calmness. Mental lightness gave Mohammed Ali his playfulness, joy and wit, and enabled him to rise to the highest levels of mastery, making him not just a boxing champion, but also an icon of an era. All three men demonstrated mental lightness as an essential component of the highest levels of mastery.

Dutch historian Johan Huizinga wrote, "With the increasing systematization and regimentation of sport, something of the pure play-quality is inevitably lost." The competitive system has drained much of the playfulness and lightness out of learning and life, making us too serious! To help my students develop mental lightness, I tell them to be *focused yet frivolous*, to not take themselves or their practice too seriously, to relax and have fun while they play. Playfulness is essential for achieving our fullest potential. To perform at our best at any level, it is important to be focused and yet also have fun. Mental lightness enables us to see the big picture while focusing on the present activity, and to react and respond more nimbly, appropriately and effectively.

Mental lightness is naturally developed in the Effortless Learning model. As we master the physical, mental, and emotional fundamentals of an activity, our insecurity and fear gradually diminish, our confidence and self-esteem grow, and we increasingly lighten up rather than tighten up.

The Stages of Non-competitive Learning

I have identified six stages in the Effortless Learning process. Because competitive ranking orders tend to be serious, I have made the categories somewhat playful. They are:

1. Way Less Than Optimal

At this beginning stage, the only pertinent skills we possess are those we have developed through other activities. With no developed skills specific to the new activity, our state is Way Less Than Optimal. How could it be any other way? If Roger Federer or Tiger Woods took up ice hockey or ballet, they would find themselves here. Depending on the amount one practices, this stage can last a minimum of several months.

2. Less Than Optimal

In this stage we have developed enough basic skill to perform the new activity at a rudimentary level. We notice and feel our improvement, and take satisfaction in it. We also recognize that true proficiency is years ahead of us. If we are honest with ourselves, this stage can last up to two years.

3. Not Bad

Here our skills have risen to a level of authentic mediocrity. Congratulations! Now we are getting somewhere! And we've put in a lot of work to get here. Here mediocre is a higher stage of development, which goes to show that everything is relative. At this point we start to believe we might have the potential to become *good*. We will be in this stage for at least several years.

4. Good

Reaching Good feels great, because it took a lot of time, practice and dedication to get here. Getting to Good means we have developed the action-specific physical skills, and also gained the self-confidence and self-esteem that come with accomplishment. If we get no further than good we have accomplished a lot. We can spend many years at this level and have a lot of fun.

5. Excellent

The shift from Good to Excellent is life changing. A vast majority of people never get to the level of good in any activity. Attaining Excellence puts us in rarified company. It yields a greater level of self-confidence and self-esteem. It also strengthens our character and becomes a healthy part of our self-identity. Reaching Excellence in any skill is always worth the time and effort.

6. Mastery

Mastery is tough to define. Call it 'excellence squared,' both in terms of skill level and all the attendant emotional, psychological and spiritual benefits. You will know it when you get there. Here all of the physical, mental, and emotional skills are indelibly etched into our cellular memory, into our psyche, even into our personality. In Mastery, we play beyond the ego level. Sustaining mastery requires continued practice, just enough to maintain the fundamentals. But attaining mastery usually includes a love of the activity for its own sake, which means "practice" is still play, still enjoyment, now done at the very highest level...the Effortless level.

6
Keys to Peak Performance

Inspiration move me brightly
Light the song with sense and color,
hold away despair
More than this I will not ask
Faced with mysteries dark and vast
— Robert Hunter

Learning to enter and stay in the zone was the original goal that led to the creation of Effortless Learning. More than thirty years later, it is still the focus of the program. The zone is the domain of peak performance. Playing in the zone is an expression of the mind/body's confidence in our mind/body skills. When *any* skill is embedded in our cellular memory, our conscious mind is freed from the need for self-conscious focus, and we are able to perform the skill effortlessly. The ability to function free of mental distractions, worry and self-conscious thinking, is what allows us to enter the zone. To do this consistently, we must be utterly convinced of the proficiency of both our practical skills, and the internal skills that I call the Keys to Peak Performance, which are presented in this chapter.

In the non-competitive Effortless Learning system, as we develop and ingrain the Keys to Peak Performance, we develop a confidence that grows and continues to deepen. Confidence is the end product of developing the following keys, not where we start. The confidence promoted in the competitive system, before we've developed our skills to the point of proficiency, is a tentative confidence. True confidence comes from doing the work and having the secure feeling that we know what we're doing. It allows us to enter the zone more frequently, and stay there longer. Such confidence is unshakable and resides at our very core as the result of mastering the following Keys to Peak Performance.

TEN KEYS TO PEAK PERFORMANCE

The Effortless Learning system describes ten *Keys to Peak Performance* that, if mastered, grant us consistent access to the zone. This system is blended together from many different sources. These keys are human qualities, and also skills or abilities that can be developed with practice. Their development allows us to fulfill our potential in any area, on and off the court, field, or stage, in the office, the classroom, the boardroom, and even the bedroom. As we develop these keys they continually enrich and enhance the quality of our lives regardless of our age, gender, beliefs, occupation, etc. Mastering these keys grounds us in the kind of abilities and self-confidence that can move mountains — and even change the world.

Great teachers have taught some or all of these keys for thousands of years. Both these keys and the whole learning process take on new significance once competition is removed; then we need to go back to the beginning and learn everything in a deeper, more efficient way. These keys are presented in a certain order. While I believe that joy, relaxation, and concentration belong at the top of the list, each person may experience these keys in a different order that is natural to their learning process.

All these keys are essential and inter-related, and we will experience and work with them repeatedly in a continuous cycle for as long as we engage in our chosen activity. In the diagram below, they are presented in the shape of an oval to demonstrate their equal importance and inter-relatedness. As I noted in Chapter 5, the keys are:

1. Joy	6. Self-motivation
2. Relaxation	7. Accountability
3. Concentration	8. Fitness
4. Patience	9. Coordination
5. Perseverance	10. Efficient skill development

The following diagram offers a visual image of the Keys to Peak Performance modules that make up Effortless Learning, with confidence in the center as the sign of our mastery.

EFFORTLESS LEARNING MODULES

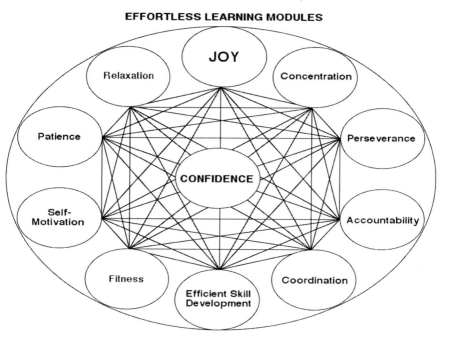

PEELING AWAY THE LAYERS

Think of each learning module as being like an onion with many layers or levels. As we work on each module over time, we become proficient in the outer layers, which peel away in succession, allowing us to progressively advance to the deeper levels of that particular quality or skill. As we develop the components of each layer, they are patterned into our cellular memory. Gradually we attain higher levels of proficiency and even mastery.

In the learning process, we return to work on each of these modules in cycles or phases, individually *and* simultaneously with all the other modules. Because they are linked together, a weakness in one module diminishes our total skill level in all areas. Periodically, after peeling away layers on individual modules, we peel away a layer on our overall development and shift to our next level or plateau. Mastery of any skill requires consistent practice and refinement of all the fundamental aspects of that skill.

In Effortless Learning, we practice these keys as they relate to our chosen activity. But these keys are universal fundamentals, life skills that relate to everything we do and are transferable to any activity. We can even develop these Keys to Peak Performance in the ordinary course of daily life, which provides countless opportunities to practice joy, relaxation, concentration, patience, perseverance, self-motivation, accountability, fitness, coordination, and efficient skill development. If we pay attention, any moment or situation may give us a chance to apply one or more of these qualities.

Because there is a great deal of information packed in each of these learning modules, it takes years to learn any module thoroughly. Each module has aspects that must be practiced specifically. Fortunately the aspects of each module partake of the other modules, so that in practicing any one module we are to some degree practicing more than one module. For example, Joy also partakes of Relaxation, Concentration, and Patience, which are all aspects or qualities of Joy. This is why I say that these modules are all inter-related.

Mastery of any skill requires mastery of all these modules simultaneously in relation to that skill. In seeking proficiency, excellence or mastery in any skill, it is essential to develop all of these keys in relation to that skill, and to do so in the ideal learning sequence outlined in previous chapters. Skipping steps is a sure path to mediocrity. Practicing steps in sequence to the point of proficiency takes longer, but it is the essence of learning and the surest path to mastery. This kind of integrated development allows us to work, play, perform and live at our peak.

The first three keys – Joy, Relaxation, and Concentration – provide a solid inner foundation for learning. Developing these skills to a high level facilitates development of all the other keys, and of any other skill we might wish to learn. For this reason I call the first three keys the Big Three.

1. JOY

Joy does not come about as the result of agreeable circumstances. Joy is, rather, a powerful and reliable cause of agreeable circumstances.
— R. Marston

How many subjects have you learned where joy was the first skill you worked on? None? Not surprising in our current environment. For many people learning has become drudgery, a chore. Since removing competition from my program I have come to see joy as the natural beginning for all learning.

To attain peak performance at anything, we have to enjoy doing it, and doing it must bring us joy. Without this, we will lack the motivation and desire to persist in developing our skills to the highest levels. Without joy, we may perform adequately or even well, but we will not fulfill our potential.

For years I taught the importance of joy in learning. But not until I witnessed Congolese master drummer Batantou Ferdinand playing at the peak of his zone did I understand that joy topped the list. It happened while I was playing percussion in a Congolese dance class with around a dozen drummers and seventy-five dancers. Batantou was the lead drummer and at the end of the two-hour class he led the drummers into the middle of the room where we continued drumming, now surrounded by the dancers. The frenetic intensity suddenly exploded to another level and we were all in the zone together. I looked at Batantou and felt incredible joy emanating from him – it seemed to be flying off him. Witnessing Batantou's joy was transformative for me, and was the catalyst for moving joy to the top of the peak performance keys.

When we first begin learning something new it can be difficult to be joyful. We haven't developed the skills to "succeed" or perform well. This lowers our chances of experiencing joy, but it doesn't have to eliminate them. Being raised in a competitive system tends to instill a false need for immediate success, for instant gratification. We want to "win" before we've even learned how to play the game. When this doesn't happen we may become frustrated, angry, or sad.

But we can practice joy from the beginning of the learning process, and even experience it in moments. Developing our joy can be as simple as remembering the feeling of a joyful experience from our past or appreciating all the things we are grateful for in life. In other words, focusing on the positives in our lives. Experiencing joy on a regular basis is our long-term goal.

We've all experienced real joy on many occasions and know how it feels on a deep level. So this is not about forcing or faking joy, but about removing the inner tensions and obstacles to joy. It is about discovering and allowing joy into the learning process. It is about weaving joy into our experience of the activity we are learning. This is easier to accomplish in a non-competitive environment where there is no external pressure to perform.

It's hard to be joyful when you're under pressure to perform and you don't know or aren't confident in what you are doing. I believe much of our inability to feel joy early in the learning process goes back to the premature introduction of competition. When you are under this pressure and you are not performing well it is impossible to feel the joy. I also believe the ways in which children are often instructed in a competitive system takes the joy out of the learning process.

In competition, we mainly associate joy with winning. We're joyful only after we have won the point, the game, the match, the meet, or the championship. In education, we generally feel joy only after acing a test (Although, sometimes we can experience great joy simply passing a test.), seeing our name on the honor roll, achieving a high GPA, receiving a diploma, or getting a bachelor's, master's, or doctorate degree. In business, joy comes after we have landed the job, made the sale, signed the contract, or received the raise, the bonus, an award or a promotion. In a competitive environment, deriving joy from the learning process rather than from the goal of winning is the exception rather than the rule. We don't often see players enjoying themselves while they are competing. It's all very serious, life and death.

Most athletes know it is possible to experience joy while hitting or kicking a ball, shooting a shot, running across a field or court, swinging a bat or club, or even just catching your breath. But we generally wait until *after* we've won to experience joy. In Effortless

Learning, we find joy in the present, not just in the moment of victory. In Effortless Tennis we experience joy at the moment we contact the ball. It is possible to experience joy in every part and activity in life. If we only experience joy after success, it is harder to enter the zone, which is itself a joyous state.

A non-competitive system enables us to relax around the learning process and have fun while developing our skills. Removing the necessity to compete and perform before we've developed sufficient skills greatly reduces needless pressure and fears of failure. This enables us to enjoy learning and to develop a genuinely joyful attitude while learning. As residual fears and inhibitions from previous learning experiences lessen over time, our skills develop more quickly, we experience more success, and our joy increases. Generally, the higher our skill level, the greater our experience of joy.

In Effortless Learning we consciously tap into and allow our natural joyfulness as we practice our chosen skill. As we "unlearn" the tension and anxiety fostered in us by the competitive system, it becomes easier to locate this natural joyfulness and incorporate it into our learning process from day one. In an ideal environment, learning something new can be fun and exciting. And we can also learn to experience joy on a more consistent basis as we learn, play, perform, work and live.

Accessing joyful states is also about learning emotional control and rewriting new healthy emotional patterns over deeply etched, counter-productive emotional responses like fear, shame and anger. It may feel like we have no control over these old, habitual responses. And we often accept them as natural, something we can't change and have to live with, like the Law of Gravity. True, we can't control our emotions all the time. But we have more control over our emotions than we think we do, or wish to admit. As Bruce Lipton's work in genetics point out, we all have the potential ability to modify, influence and change our emotional responses over time. But this takes practice.

By monitoring our emotional state we can sense when we are moving into less-than-optimal territory and begin to affect a change in our response. Once we understand that negative responses such as fear and anger limit our performance we can begin to undo those old patterns by developing new healthy habits in their place. From the first days in the program, the Effortless Learning process works to affect significant changes in our habitual emotional responses.

Not surprisingly, putting joy at the top of the Keys to Peak Performance has brought a great deal of joy to my Effortless Learning program. When I see students getting serious and upset with themselves, I'll ask, "How's your joy factor?" or "Are you feeling the joy?" Since they understand the importance of joy in the learning process, these simple reminders are usually enough to get them to lighten up by the time the next ball arrives. And they generally have more fun. So remember the joy factor, and see that it is possible to experience more joy in all aspects of your life.

2. RELAXATION

Relaxation is essential to learning, performing, competing and living. The health benefits of relaxation, and its importance to peak performance, are by now common knowledge. Innumerable studies on muscle tightness as it relates to reaction time show that reaction time is faster when muscles are relaxed, and slower when they are tense. Mental relaxation allows us to see and assess situations more quickly and clearly, which also increases our reaction/response time. These facts are why relaxation is number two in the keys to peak performance.

World-renowned track star, Carl Lewis, after finishing second in the hundred-meter dash at the 1988 Olympics, was asked why he lost. Lewis said that his opponent won because he was able to relax down the straightaway. Even while running as fast as humanly possible in a ten-second sprint, these top athletes are trying to relax.

Relaxation is a physical and mental skill that requires practice to learn. Until we learn this skill we don't really know how to relax in the fullest sense. When we master this skill, we can relax in competition, and even in high-stress situations. This is a healthier, more effective response than the fight-or-flight response usually triggered automatically by the limbic or "reptilian" brain in response to stress.

From my observations, few people have highly developed relaxation skills, and most are quite tense. The competitive system makes us uptight. You often hear coaches exhorting their players to relax, but when your ego and self-esteem are on the line it is not easy to be relaxed, unless you are supremely confident in your skills, and you have consciously developed the skill of relaxation.

The first step in learning relaxation is unlearning tension. This takes time and practice. After eighteen years of highly competitive tennis, it took me four years in a non-competitive environment to begin to comprehend the true depth of relaxation we can attain. First, we need to experience what complete relaxation feels like with no competition — to know it in our cells. If we can't relax when there is no pressure, how are we going to be able to relax under pressure?

Effortless Learning teaches relaxation from day one in the nurturing confines of a cooperative learning environment. In my beginner tennis program I have students start by bouncing a ball with their racquets. After a few minutes I ask them to repeat the exercise and see if they can perform the same action in a more relaxed manner. All of them acknowledge feeling more relaxed when they are finished. While learning basic skills and repetitive drills, they also learn to perform each task in a relaxed manner. Over the course of the first year, students play in an increasingly relaxed state. They can feel the difference. By practicing relaxation, we are patterning that response into our cellular memory.

Many books teach relaxation, and I highly recommend finding a good one and developing this essential skill. Other methods for developing relaxation skills are stretching, breathing, and meditation. Different activities allow us to learn how to relax in slightly different yet similar ways.

My experience drumming has taught me much about relaxation in the absence of competition. Relaxation is essential in high level drumming, where at certain times you're required to play continuously at a fast pace for as long as two hours without stopping. If you don't relax completely, your muscles seize up and you can't continue for that long.

Many people associate relaxing with being lazy or "spacing out". But the kind of relaxation I'm talking about has nothing to do with being lazy or "spacing out". It is in fact a high-level, highly prized *skill* cultivated by people at the top of their fields. The more relaxed we are, the more aware and effective we are in action. When my students comment that they were "too relaxed" I tell them, "You can't be too relaxed, you just lost focus." Initially it is easy to loose focus when we start to relax. But eventually we can learn to be focused and relaxed simultaneously. Skilled relaxation involves a conscious awareness of the body, a noticing and releasing of tension. It loosens the muscles, calms the mind, and heightens awareness. The ability to remain relaxed under pressure leads to peak performance. It also allows us to enjoy, and find joy in, the present activity.

An essential component of relaxation is breathing. Skillful breathing can mean the difference between playing or performing well, and being in the zone. Many disciplines – sports, yoga and meditation, music and more – recognize the connection between breathing, relaxation, and peak performance. Skillful breathing efficiently conducts and conserves our energy, oxygenates our blood, muscles and brain, and changes our state of consciousness. The problem is that most of us have never learned efficient breathing, and have ingrained less-than-optimal breathing patterns into our cellular memory. For example, the common habit of holding our breath when we feel stress, the startle response, increases tension and translates into numerous activities. We may hold our breath and tense up when we are hitting a ball, learning new dance moves, taking an exam, going out on a date, or closing an important business deal. All nervous tension drains our energy, lowers our performance, and tires us out.

Holding our breath, or shallow breathing unconsciously creates tension and inhibits free flowing movement and clear thinking. It inhibits physical action by tightening too many muscles at a critical time. It inhibits performance by keeping us in states of anxiety, uncertainty, confusion or fear – i.e., in fight-or-flight mode. Playing, working, or performing in these states uses up far more energy than we use when performing optimally, with a relaxed body and mind, and regulated breath. Imagine again the contorted faces of little children running a race. Efficient breathing helps us relax and conserve energy, allowing us to move into a meditative state and more easily enter the zone.[1]

---

[1] In the last chapter I talked about conscious/subconscious learning. Breathing is a good example of this process. To make a change in our breathing patterns, we first have to be aware of our current breathing habits, and then learn new ones. Through practice, our new breathing habits become natural, automatic,

Today, fifteen years after removing competition from the Effortless Tennis program, I am still experiencing new levels of both physical and psychological relaxation.

3.CONCENTRATION

To be here now and enjoy the present moment is our most important task.
Thich Nhat Hanh

Concentration is the ability to focus exclusive attention on one object or activity for a sustained period in the midst of potential distractions. Think of a cat stalking a bird, a dog watching the ball in its owner's hand before the throw, or two Samurai warriors facing one another over their drawn swords, each knowing that to yield to distraction for an instant could mean death. This is the level of concentration that allows us to achieve peak performance in any skill. Unlike the samurai, our lives aren't on the line when we practice concentration in our chosen skills. But being raised in a competitive system, our egos and our self-esteem usually are. While competing, winning and losing can feel like life and death, engaging our fight-or-flight responses.

Concentration is a skill to be developed like any other. It is also an essential skill that, perhaps more than any other key, enables us to learn and develop all other skills. It is the ability to focus our attention

---

and effortless. In Effortless Tennis, we learn to start inhaling gently at the moment our partner (formerly our adversary) contacts the ball. We continue to inhale until we softly exhale, as if we are blowing out just one candle, as we make contact with the ball. We learn to exhale precisely at the moment of contact, not just before or just after. We continue exhaling until our partner again contacts the ball, when we again begin to inhale. When we're inhaling, it aids us in keeping our attention focused solely on the ball, and it feels like our inhalation is drawing the ball to us. A golfer would inhale on her backswing and exhale at contact. A basketball player would inhale as they go up to shoot the ball and exhale at the moment they release the ball. By focusing on our breathing we occupy our conscious mind, thereby getting out of our own way and enabling our body to do what we have programmed it to do. This breathing pattern allows us to access the zone where we will play "out of our minds." Whatever your activity, experiment to see how breathing might best apply.

on an activity or subject and make sense of it, understand it, and learn it. Almost everything we do requires some degree of concentration.

Practicing concentration is practicing being in the present moment with focused awareness. The present is the only moment where we have any control or power in life. The present is the only place where we can learn because it is the only place where we can be aware. To practice being present with focused awareness, it helps to be relaxed and to enjoy the moment. Our ability to concentrate and learn is enhanced by relaxation and enjoyment. Since joy, relaxation and concentration are inextricably linked and mutually supportive, it helps to practice all three together.

People often distract themselves from the present by thinking about or worrying over the past or future. In tennis, this often takes the form of ruminating about a previous shot missed or game lost, or about a next shot we might miss or game we might lose. In practicing concentration, we accept and let go of whatever has happened, and relax and focus on what is happening now. This also helps us avoid worrying about the future. We can't go back in time to change any outcome, and we can't function at our peak by worrying about the future.

Another common distraction to concentration is negative or self-critical thinking and the emotions they trigger. Being relaxed and focusing on what is happening now, and enjoying the moment as best we can, is also the solution. We only have power and can affect change in the present.

Because concentration is required to learn any skill, learning any skill develops our concentration. There is also a direct correlation between level of concentration and level of performance. In Effortless Learning we practice the fundamentals (emotional and mental as well as physical) of a particular skill in cycles over time, gradually attaining deeper levels of mastery. This naturally develops and hones our concentration, because in practicing fundamentals we're simultaneously developing our ability to stay focused in the present.

It is impossible to develop our concentration skills to the highest level necessary for peak performance if we do not have the physical fundamentals of our activity programmed into our cellular memory. Only after patterning the movements we need to execute into our cells will we be able to fully develop our ability to stay focused in the present while performing the activity, especially in competition. Once the physical skills are ingrained, our concentration level will soar. We will be able to perform the actions without having to think about them. This holds true no matter what we are working on.

So whether it is learning the scales in music or learning how to dribble with both hands in basketball or both feet in soccer, until we can virtually "do it in our sleep" we won't be able to perform at our peak. As with joy and relaxation, it is easier to stay focused in the present when there is no pressure, no competition. Even without competition in the learning process, developing great concentration is a long-term project.

4. PATIENCE

The Miriam Webster Dictionary defines *patience* as "bearing pains or trials calmly or without complaint; manifesting forbearance under provocation or strain; steadfast despite opposition, difficulty, or adversity." My favorite definition of patience is "the ability to suppress annoyance when confronted with delay." As a teenager I had a large poster on my wall that showed two buzzards out in the dessert sitting on the branch of a dead tree, with a skeleton of a cow in the foreground. Buzzards are scavengers and therefore only eat dead animals. The caption to this poster had one of the buzzards saying to the other, "Patience my ass, I'm gonna kill something." When we lose our patience, it can feel as if we want to do something completely outside of our nature, something unnatural, because we are frustrated. Unfortunately, rarely does this approach work.

We have all heard that saying, "Patience is a virtue." But patience is more than a virtue; it's an essential key to life. I've heard many people state, "I have no patience." Without patience, we can't fully enjoy, relax, concentrate or persist in learning and developing any skill to the level of excellence. Patience is the antidote to frustration. It is an emotional skill that allows us to stay with and even profit from a present activity we may not be enjoying in the moment.

Effortless Learning recognizes that doing the work required to hone our skills to a high degree requires a great deal of patience. So it emphasizes patience as an essential skill to be learned while learning the more "practical" skills of an activity. *When patience is taught from the very beginning of the learning process as an essential skill, children are able to accept this and learn it relatively effortlessly.* It is much harder for adults already raised in a competitive system to learn patience, as frustration and impatience are so often etched into their cellular memory relative to the learning process.

Perhaps a quarter of the adults who come to my Effortless Tennis program exhibit a solid level of patience when they arrive. These are usually people who have developed another activity to a high level, and so have developed patience in the process. Many of the adults who haven't developed patience in other areas stick with the program and learn patience as they learn the game. But a certain percentage drop out due to frustration with not improving as fast as they would like to, not having as much fun as they hoped, or from simple frustration with the learning process itself. In other words, from lack of patience.

Patience is a non-optional part of Effortless Learning. We especially need it as we move along the learning plateaus, which takes time, practice, effort and sustained focus. Once we understand the nature of the learning process, with all that it requires of us and gives to us, we become more willing to exercise and develop patience. And this allows us to develop the next key – Perseverence!

5. PERSEVERANCE

High-level skill takes years to develop, often longer than we wish. This is where perseverance comes in. Patience, a relatively passive quality, allows us to endure frustration and difficulty without reacting negatively. Perseverance, a more dynamic quality, allows us to persist in an action in the face of obstacles that would otherwise turn us away. Perseverance is essential to learning any specialized skill because the "learning curve" that is an integral part of such a process is inherently frustrating, especially in a competitive environment, and often makes us want to stop or give up altogether before we attain proficiency.

To achieve any high-level goal or skill requires perseverance in motivation, in focus, and in practice. We must persevere in those phases when we're not "feeling the joy," and don't seem to be making any progress. In such periods, perseverance in our practice often entails "going through the motions" when we don't feel motivated. This is what it can feel like when we are on a plateau. In such times it helps to remember that by going through the motions, literally, we are continuing to etch and integrate new knowledge and deeper levels of skill and ability into our cellular memory. As we rise to higher levels, it seems like things should get easier, and in certain ways this is true. Yet the higher our skill level, the more subtle the information we are integrating, and the longer it takes to get to the next levels. For this reason, perseverance is, in a way, the backbone of mastery.

6. SELF-MOTIVATION

This key is an evolutionary step up from concentration, patience and perseverance. Self-motivation, a dynamic *and* proactive quality, allows us to persist through all obstacles *until we reach our goal*. It is *the* key that separates mediocrity from excellence in almost every field of endeavor. People may help, encourage and support us on our journey through life. But no one else's support, love or faith in us can substitute for our commitment, determination, hard work and persistence over the years that it takes to achieve excellence and mastery. Not even luck, intelligence, good genes and natural talent can make up for a lack of self-motivation. Countless gifted people settle for "less than their best" while their less gifted peers persevere in developing their abilities to reach the top of their fields.

I finally fully appreciated the importance of self-motivation in my late twenties when I decided to dramatically improve my tennis game. My motivation was to reach my highest level as a player and as a teacher. I knew that in order to teach at a world-class level I needed to develop my game to that level. To do this I devised an accelerated training regime consisting of a minimum of four hours of practice a day in two two-hour sessions. I had been teaching and playing locally for many years and had many potential practice partners. Getting one session a day was no problem. The challenge was to find a partner for my second practice session each day, five or six days a week, for six months. I had to make it happen. No one was going to do it for me. It took a great deal of self-motivation. The result of this self-motivation was that my skills rose to the highest level of my life.

Self-motivation is in some ways easier in a competitive

environment, due to the lure of victory and the ever-present threat of failure. The fear of losing and the desire to win have always been powerful motivating forces in human endeavor. But by themselves, for all of the reasons described in previous chapters, these competitive factors are not enough to motivate us in developing our skills to their fullest potential. The highest levels of self-motivation come from our love or passion for an activity, and a desire for the joy, satisfaction and self-esteem that true mastery brings. These are the qualities we develop in a non-competitive learning environment.

7. ACCOUNTABILITY

An obligation or willingness to accept
responsibility or to account for one's actions.
Meriam Webster's Dictionary

All of the skills so far could be called "inner skills", qualities that do not depend upon physical skill and ability. Together they comprise a healthy mental, emotional and spiritual framework for living and learning any skill. They are also marks of human maturity. Accountability is perhaps the pinnacle of such maturity. Here we take responsibility for our actions and the results they produce, good, bad and ugly. We don't let ourselves off the hook with excuses. We don't blame someone else for our problems. Making excuses easily becomes a habitual response etched in our cellular memory. It is more common than you might think.

The problem with excuses, even "good" ones, is that they generally "explain" a problem without leading to a solution by assigning our "failure" to something outside ourselves over which we have no control. Being accountable means shouldering the responsibility for our own actions, behavior and development, and consistently acting in a manner that will produce the results we want to achieve.

Over the thirty-plus years that I have been teaching tennis, I have heard every excuse imaginable given for less than optimal performance. I have developed what I call the "excuse pile." Where I live and teach the dominant geographical feature is Mount Tamalpais, which towers over the area. Mt. Tam is our excuse pile. When students make excuses while practicing I tell them to " put it on the pile." This way they are able to let go of the excuse and get back to developing their skills. When students become truly accountable, their excuses are left on the pile, and their practice and their progress become more consistent. In the Effortless Learning model, accountability is a quality that must be developed through persistent practice.

Being accountable for our actions is empowering because it is based in the recognition that we are indeed responsible for our actions, our efforts, and our progress. Making excuses gives our power away by assigning blame for less than optimal performance to outer circumstances, people, parents, the weather, a bad day, the "tennis gods", etc. Some excuses may be true to some degree. But in the end, our level of skill and ability in any area is determined by how much time, energy and dedication we put into it. In this sense, in regard to our skill in our chosen field, we do create our own reality. Understanding and accepting this fact, and applying it in principle, is the essence of accountability. And it will, as much as any other key, help us achieve our goals.

8. Fitness

Fitness, a key factor in any physical activity, is essential to achieving peak performance. Even our non-physical skills benefit when we are in good physical condition, which enhances our mental faculties, balances our emotions and generally improves our energy level, our confidence and self-esteem. There are three components to fitness: physical, mental, and emotional. Peak performance in physical skills such as water polo, karate, ballet, mountain climbing, etc., requires great physical conditioning. Peak performance in mental skills such as chess, debating, math, science, etc., takes great mental fitness. Peak performance in emotional arenas, as in relationships, parenting, or being a good therapist or coach, requires great emotional fitness, or emotional maturity. The ideal is to be fit in all three areas.

Research shows that physical fitness improves our mental and emotional fitness and our overall well-being. To achieve fitness, it helps to find a form of exercise you enjoy, start out slowly, gradually increasing the intensity and duration of the activity as your conditioning improves, and avoid pushing your body beyond a healthy limit. Most people push to hard in the beginning and end up quitting because it is not enjoyable. Some people push themselves too hard over time and injure themselves or burn out. A healthy medium is best for most people.

Mental and emotional fitness are more subtle and in some ways more challenging than physical fitness. Our competitive system has focused on mental fitness with its primary emphasis on winning at all cost, but it has seriously undervalued emotional fitness. I have found a lack of emotional fitness to be a significant barrier to many individuals in the early phases of learning. The phenomenon of top professional athletes, extraordinarily fit physically and mentally in terms of their sports performance, self-sabotaging and self-destructing due to lack of emotional maturity, highlights the importance of this undervalued key. There is a virtual epidemic in professional sports of players with a serious deficit in emotional fitness. Effortless Learning emphasizes emotional fitness from the beginning, as an essential component not only of the learning process, but of true excellence and mastery as well. In fact, the first seven keys are all components of emotional fitness.

9. COORDINATION

Like fitness, coordination comes in three forms: physical, mental, and emotional, all of which can be developed and improved with practice.

Physical coordination is essential for physical activities such as sports, dance, music, the martial arts and more. Mental coordination or dexterity is also essential for high-level physical performance where assessments, decisions and actions are often required in fractions of a second. It is also essential to more obviously mental activities like mathematics, accounting, science, engineering, law, chess, etc. Emotional coordination or facility is also helpful in physical skills and activities. It allows us to sense the emotional states of others – friends, coaches, partners or opponents – and coordinate or adapt our own emotional responses to the needs of the moment. It is also essential in activities like teaching, acting, therapy, mentoring, politics, sales, and other arenas where relationship is the medium of "performance".

Many people assume that coordination is something we either have or not, that it's not learnable. But through practice and repetition, most people can, if sufficiently motivated, develop the necessary degree of all three levels of coordination required to achieve excellence in any field. Like any skill, it comes down to desire, commitment, self-motivation and practice.

When I was nine, my dad put down a load of small stones along the path that led to our mailbox to prevent the area from getting muddy when it rained. One day I got a small baseball bat about two feet long and an inch in diameter and started hitting the stones into an empty field. At first I missed far more than I hit. But after a while I started getting the feeling of it and made contact much more frequently. By the time my dad had to bring in another load of stones to cover the path, I had gotten very good at hitting the stones. So my great hand-eye coordination isn't a quality I was born with or a gift from God. It's something I worked to develop, a skill etched through practice into my cellular memory.

I've discovered through teaching tennis that coordination can be learned by almost anyone at any age. Many people are uncoordinated not because they have no aptitude for coordination, but because they never developed their coordination. Their lack of coordination became part of their cellular memory. Many of my students come to the courts with less-than-optimal coordination and, within a few months to years, become very coordinated and skilled tennis players. They have simply etched new patterns of coordination into their cellular memory while developing new physical skills. It's not magic — it's practice.

10. EFFICIENT SKILL DEVELOPMENT

Achieving excellence in any skill requires efficiency in performing the fundamentals of that activity. Increasing efficiency in the fundamentals is the key to mastery. This is the simple philosophy of Effortless Learning. In tennis, different players may have different styles of hitting and moving. But the best players, regardless of their style, perform with an efficiency developed through years of training. There are more efficient ways to move to and hit a ball. Efficiency is what allows us to consistently and successfully execute necessary actions or tasks with a minimum waste of time, movement, and energy.

Mechanics — how we perform an essential action — is a matter of simple physics applied within the rules and logic of our chosen activity. The mechanics or applied physics of any activity allow us to achieve maximum power, control and efficiency in that activity. The mechanics of Aikido or Jujitsu allow a smaller, weaker individual to throw or disarm a much larger, stronger person. In tennis, if we can move our body into the ideal position as the ball approaches, move our racquet back in an efficient, fluid motion, and forward again to meet the ball, simultaneously transferring our body weight completely into the ball as we complete our stroke, we will hit an incredibly powerful shot that feels effortless.

Efficient mechanics are something we continue to develop as long as we play our particular "game". Over the years, as our movements and actions become more efficient and more deeply patterned into our cellular memory, we will continue to shave fractions of seconds off our preparation and reaction time, our skills will continue to improve, and our execution will become increasingly effortless.

Effortless Learning focuses on efficient skill development from the beginning, and works to increase efficiency through all the phases of participation. It does this whether we practice four hours a day, or two hours twice a week. It is a long-term learning model that allows individuals to develop solid foundation skills in their chosen activity, and if they persist over time, to attain excellence and even mastery.

PLAYING IN THE ZONE OF LIFE

Achieving excellence or mastery in any activity is a great accomplishment in life. In Effortless Learning our potential for such accomplishment increases as we develop these ten Keys to Peak Performance while learning the more practical skills of our chosen activity. Effortless Learning in any arena is a lifelong and life-changing process. As we're able to bring more joy, relaxation, and concentration into our lives, our lives will be more effortless. As we're able to show more patience and perseverance, and greater self-motivation and accountability, our lives will be more effortless. As we develop our fitness and coordination, as our skills become more efficient, and our confidence grows, our lives will be more effortless. As our lives become more effortless, it becomes possible to dream the big dreams, and then realize them — whether these dreams are personal or planetary.

PART FOUR
The Next Step in Human Evolution

Let my inspiration flow
In token lines suggesting rhythm
That will not forsake me
Till my tale is told and done
While the firelight's aglow
Strange shadows from the flames will grow
Till things we've never seen
Will seem familiar
— Robert Hunter

7

Toward a More Cooperative
Worldview

*Those who say it cannot be done
should not interrupt the people doing it.*
— Chinese proverb

If you've read this far, you now have a basic grasp of the fundamental principles of Effortless Learning. You can even start putting these principles into practice in your chosen field or activity, and in your life. If you persevere in this, you will experience steady growth over time, and eventually attain mastery. Any individual, with the perspectives and information in this book, can make the shift from a competitive to a non-competitive model. But how do we bring the benefits of this non-competitive model of learning to a society that is largely defined by competition?

COMPETITION, COOPERATION, RECIPROCATION

Political scientist Robert Axelrod, in his book *The Evolution of Cooperation,* posed a similar question when he asked, "How can cooperation emerge in a world of egoists without central authority?" Seeking an answer, Axelrod devised a series of computer tournaments, with three strategies or options that each player could employ. The first option was to compete against the other player(s). The second was to cooperate with them. The third was to reciprocate with them.

In analyzing the results of the tournaments Axelrod discovered that the simplest of all the strategies — reciprocating — produced the best outcome. He called this strategy *tit for tat.* The tit-for-tat strategy entails cooperating on the first move in the game, and then cooperating or competing, depending on the play of the other player, on his or her next move. If the other player's move is cooperative, then we reciprocate with a cooperative move. If the other player's move is competitive, we react competitively.

In every tournament, this tit-for-tat strategy produced the best results for all participants. Axelrod then developed a mathematical analysis to show how cooperation based upon reciprocity can emerge in a population of egoists with only a small cluster of reciprocators, *and then resist invasion by competitive strategies.* In other words, for the purposes of our current analysis, if enough people agree to cooperate, it won't matter if everyone cooperates; cooperation will still work on a large scale.

One of the most important conclusions of Axelrod's study is that nice guys can finish first. But he knew the shift from competition to cooperation wouldn't happen overnight. He concluded, "cooperation based upon reciprocity can emerge and prove stable provided the shadow of the future is long enough." In other words, it's possible to evolve into a more cooperative species, but it's going to take time.

Another study conducted by Robert Kurzban of the University of Pennsylvania, and Daniel Houser of George Mason University, verified Axelrod's findings. Kurzban and Houser found that no matter what the strategy — whether you were a cooperator, a competitor, or a reciprocator — all three strategies (cooperation, competition, and reciprocation) had statistically similar payoffs. In other words, it didn't matter the strategy; the results were the same over the long term. This result of no statistical difference occurred when there were the three choices of strategies. If you were always competing in your decisions no matter whether the other player competed or cooperated, you either won big or lost big. If you were always cooperating, the result was the same whether the other player was cooperating or competing: win big or lose big.

But while the statistical results in terms of winning and losing were the same with mutual reciprocation, there was a difference. With reciprocation, the payoff and the loss were often not as large. There was a significant decrease in big winners and big losers. This brings up the question: Is that a bad thing, or a good thing? A competitive mindset might view it as a bad thing, while a non-competitive mindset might view it as a good thing. But if we look at the world today, with its small fraction of "winners" – the millionaires and billionaires – and its overwhelming percentage of "losers" – those who live in poverty, 25% of whom earn less than a dollar a day – it begins to look like a good thing after all. Then cooperation does appear to offer a solution to many of the world's problems.

These studies clearly show the negative effects of a tit-for-tat strategy when both sides are competing against each other – big losers. In a competitive model, there really is no choice, no option other than competition. And we're not just talking about games, sports or business. Competition is often devastating when it is applied to political and social problems, because it provokes rather than resolves conflict. The Protestant/Catholic conflict in Ireland, the Israeli/Palestinian conflict in the Middle East, the Hutu/Tutsi conflict in Rwanda all demonstrate the futility of the competitive model for solving human and social problems. Mahatma Gandhi made this point when he said, "An eye for an eye only ends up making the whole world blind."

Tit-for-tat cooperation points the way to a brighter future.

EVOLVING VIEWS

While the competitive system still reigns supreme, there are signs that people are waking up to the need for more cooperative models. Let's look at just a few instances in which normally competitive entities are moving toward greater cooperation.

The European Union

Established in 1992, the European Union is a confederation of 27 countries coming together to cooperate in politics, agriculture, and economic policy. While there is still a great deal of dissension and disagreement within the Union, it is a positive sign that most of the countries of Europe have formed a cooperative alliance after hundreds of years as adversaries.

Education

Education has traditionally entailed a high degree of competition, not only among students, but also among institutions competing for prestige, funding and students. Each year *Newsweek* magazine announces its rankings of top universities.

The good news is that many academicians are beginning to understand the advantages of cooperation. One of myriad examples is the Committee on Institutional Cooperation, an academic consortium of the Big Ten Universities plus the University of Chicago. This organization is committed to "advancing academic excellence through resource sharing and collaboration."

Competitive education is the most common form of education around the world. But the highly successful Montessori and Waldorf schools offer a superb and well-rounded curriculum in a non-competitive structure. Some of the brightest minds of our time have started out in these schools, which have been around for ninety and eighty years respectively, and have thousands of campuses throughout the world. By learning together in a cooperative environment we learn to respect one another and our individual viewpoints.

The Linux Model

Business has long practiced cutthroat competition, a survival-of-the-fittest winner-take-all approach. But there has been an increasing shift in parts of the business community toward greater cooperation, with various motives, whether to cut costs, expand territory, increase profits, best other competitors, improve production, and more.

Also, a revolutionary new cooperative model is emerging in business, advanced by Linux, an enormously successful computer operating systems designer. Incredibly, Linux has *no central company and no company headquarters*. Linux open-source systems are developed and improved by thousands of volunteers, and by workers for giant computer companies such as IBM, Hewlett-Packard, and Intel. These latter companies actually pay their employees to improve another company's product.

Equally remarkable is that Linux doesn't compete against other companies, nor hide its system's "secrets", a standard business practice. The Linux system and design data are offered free to all, and new versions are sent out regularly to anyone interested in improving it. Participating individuals and companies profit from this improvement in various ways while working together to continually improve a product that is, as a result, more reliable with fewer bugs. While anyone can obtain basic copies of Linux for free, distributors, computer makers, and software companies find ways to profit from their association with Linux.

This remarkable cooperative model, unimaginable ten years ago, gives Linux access to a pool of talent, ingenuity and expertise no conventional company could bring together or afford. Linux is immune to "the competition" because it doesn't compete. Yet the competition is apparently vulnerable to Linux, which is reportedly cutting into the profits of Microsoft. And while Microsoft resorts to pressuring its users to keep them from going with Linux, Linux just keeps doing what it is doing – putting out an ever-better product. This new business model is one of the exciting beacons demonstrating the emergence of a new cooperative paradigm.

The Internet

The World Wide Web is one of the best contemporary examples of a successfully functioning, free, cooperative communication system. It has already been adapted to business, politics, social interaction, education and much more. The Web has proven the viability, effectiveness and power of cooperation as a means of achieving what no single individual, corporation, or even nation can achieve alone through competition.

In just a few short years, through the literal interconnectedness provided by the Internet, individuals and groups around the world now serve as beacons of light and hope, providing inspiration, information and support to one another. It has arguably changed the world more in a shorter period of time than any other invention in history. And it continues to draw the largest pool of volunteer participants who are making it all that it is today, and evolving it into whatever it will be tomorrow.

Effortless Tennis

It has been my joy and privilege to create a successful, effective learning program, based in cooperation, in the highly competitive game of tennis. As I write these words seventeen years after making the shift to a non-competitive model, my program is alive and well. Hundreds of people who have been through my program are enjoying the camaraderie of being partners instead of opponents while together they develop the skills of the game they love and fulfill their potential. If non-competitive learning didn't work, I would have been out of business long ago. I hope more teachers will take up the challenge of adopting the approach of Effortless Learning in their instruction.

THE LAST BASTION

The last bastion of the competitive paradigm to evolve into healthy cooperation will be the one most entrenched in competition. That would be politics, where the game is power. At every level of politics, from local to national to international, competitors engage in conflict to defeat one another for the prize of power and prestige. Their weapons range from words, attack ads and propaganda campaigns, to varied covert acts of sabotage, to legal and economic sanctions, to wars. In our time we have seen the competitive politics of negativity and attack degenerate at every level, dividing and driving our nation and our world deeper into seemingly unresolvable and catastrophic conflicts.

As more people recognize the futility of competition as a solution to our varied human problems, they will begin to see the wisdom and necessity of cooperation instead. And as more people shift to a cooperative mindset, they will elect politicians with a similar vision. But it will take a significant shift to a cooperative model for all parties to truly work together for the greater good to solve our collective problems, many of which are a result of our flawed competitive system.

GETTING UNSTUCK FROM THE PAST

Our competitive behavior has been hard-wired into our cellular memory for so long it seems there is nothing we can do to change.

Fortunately, it is always possible to create new positive patterns in our cellular memory that will, in time, override old destructive patterns. But this requires awareness, and a will to change. For groups, nations and our species to change and evolve to a higher level, it will require collective awareness and a collective will to change.

A thought-provoking episode from the television series *Star Trek: The Next Generation* begins with the crew of the Enterprise locked in a desperate battle that ends with the Enterprise exploding. Suddenly, the crew is back in the same situation, and the Enterprise explodes again. Once again they are in the same situation, with the same result. They are stuck in a time loop. Eventually the crew starts having memories of this scenario having played itself out before. Now each time the loop begins, they figure out a little more of what is happening and how to solve it. They begin making slightly different decisions to see if it changes the outcome. For a while there is no change; the Enterprise continues to be destroyed. Finally, they change a seemingly insignificant decision that had been overlooked each time before, and that small change allows them to survive.

I believe our species is caught in a similar kind of loop with our competitive behavior. We have been competing against one another forever, with many destructive consequences that include limited development, poverty, racism, and war. We've also, very slowly, been making different choices trying to remedy the human problems mentioned above. But the one thing we haven't yet tried is shifting from the competitive model that we've always relied on for survival, to a non-competitive/cooperative model. As a result, we haven't been able to evolve emotionally, psychologically or behaviorally beyond the competitive mentality, which always sees "others" as adversaries.

I believe that a non-competitive educational system will lead the way to a transformation in human consciousness. I have seen many adults in my tennis program shift to a more cooperative worldview. I believe that people are very concerned about the direction our world is headed and are ready to make significant changes to alter our current course. However, raising a generation of children with a cooperative mindset and worldview will be easier and more effective than trying to change generations of people entrenched in an outdated paradigm. As Nobel Prize winning scientist, Max Plank observed, "A new scientific truth does not triumph by convincing its opponents and making them see the light, but rather because its opponents eventually die, and a new generation grows up that is familiar with it"

8
Actualizing Our Potential

I wake up every morning with a clearer dream.
I see happy, healthy children, educated with plenty of food to eat.
I see a world living in peace and prosperity.
I see broken things fixed and all fears set free.
Guess that lady ain't so crazy 'cause I'm starting to believe,
Every day now I'm planting a seed — a new imagination.
— Don Carlisle

While doing research for this book, I was led to the work of two great psychologists in whose work and insights I found confirmation for my own notions about Effortless Learning. The first is Alfred Adler, whose therapeutic approach helps individuals connect with all of humanity on an equal and cooperative footing. Adler's technique focuses on three therapeutic processes:

1. Reducing painful, exaggerated feelings of inferiority to a normal size that can be used to spur psychological growth and development, and a healthy striving for significance;

2. Redirecting energy and attention away from a useless and corrosive striving for superiority over others, and toward more useful and cooperative ends; and

3. Fostering feelings of equality and community.

I believe Adler's approach contains the essentials of Evolutionary Education that, if applied, could greatly benefit individuals and society as a whole. Feelings of inferiority, a useless and corrosive striving for superiority over others, and a resulting lack of a sense of equality and community keep us stuck in our current reality. We need a new vision and a new approach.

When I speak of reducing feelings of inferiority, I refer to the countless people who have been emotionally, psychologically and spiritually harmed by the competitive system described in these pages. As we have seen, these negative effects include low self-esteem, timidity, feelings of inferiority, procrastination, fear of taking risks, and more. And all of them limit our well-being, our human development, our capacity to contribute to society, and our enjoyment of life. Adler and others I have mentioned in these pages point to an approach that would encourage and raise the self-esteem of the majority, and give everyone a chance to shine.

The second key figure in whose ideas I have found much confirmation is psychologist Abraham Maslow. We will be taking a closer look at his insights in this chapter.

THE HIERARCHY OF NEEDS

Maslow created a perceptive model of human development based in a *hierarchy of needs*. His model showed how our basic needs must be met before higher needs can take precedence in our lives. For example, our need for food and drink is more basic than our need for love and esteem, which are higher in the hierarchy of needs. To the degree that we are starving or thirsty, love and esteem become less significant. But, once fed and our thirst slaked, our attention and energy may turn to higher needs for love, esteem, peace of mind, and so forth.

This parallels Effortless Learning's Fundamentals of Learning, with its sequence, or necessary hierarchy in the learning process, where fundamentals must be grasped before attempting to learn higher, more complex elements. In the processes of learning and of human development, there are essential and natural sequences to be followed in order to obtain the best results.

Maslow's model is presented as a pyramid of five distinct levels of need in a clear developmental order. The five levels of this pyramid, from the base to the peak, are as follows: 1) Physiological needs. 2) Needs for safety and security. 3) Needs for love and belonging. 4) The need for esteem. 5) The need for self-actualization. Below is a brief description of each in turn.

1. Physiological Needs

This level addresses the basic needs required for bodily survival. These include the need for oxygen, water, food, warmth, sleep, and so forth. These essential needs must be met before we can pursue higher needs. Once they are met, a second tier of needs comes into play.

2. Safety and Security Needs

Here our focus shifts to finding safe surroundings, physical security, and protection from danger. Before these needs are met we live in states of anxiety and fear, unable to pursue higher needs. Mankind lived for thousands of years at these first two levels. And a large percentage of the world's population is still stuck at this level, living from day to day focused on meeting the needs of these first two tiers. When our physiological and safety/security needs are met, and are no longer matters of urgency, our focus naturally shifts to the third tier.

3. Love and Belonging Needs

Here our energy and focus shifts to the realm of relations, to our needs for social and intimate connections with family, friends, lovers, children, and community. We humans are social and emotional animals. We hunger for connection, for interaction with one another. We long to belong, to feel a part of a family or community. The need for love, for human connection, for acceptance and belonging, are a biologically hardwired feature of our humanity. And until these needs are met, we cannot fully be at home in our own skin, become whole, or evolve beyond this third tier.

4. Esteem Needs

Maslow noted two levels of esteem needs – external and internal. In the external level we seek esteem outside of ourselves, from others, in the form of attention, approval, recognition, respect, status, authority, fame, glory, etc. This level is linked to our competitive strivings.

The internal level includes the need for self-respect, competence, confidence, self-mastery, and other qualities that can only be found within. Internal esteem needs cannot be met by external recognition or rewards. They are a sign of psychological health and maturity, the fruits of a healthy relationship with our self, with others and with life. We alone know when we have met these needs, and we know that no one outside of ourselves can meet them for us.

5. Self-Actualization

The fifth level of Maslow's hierarchy of needs involves what we call the spiritual. Here we have an ongoing desire to be our best, to fulfill our potential in the deepest, truest sense. We feel an urge to know ourselves from the core of our being, and to live the very highest standard of conduct in our actions in the world of relations as human personalities.

A partial list of qualities that define a self-actualized person include awareness, clear perception of reality, moral and ethical behavior, honesty, a philosophical sense of humor (i.e. playfulness), social interest, deep interpersonal relationships, freedom, independence, effortlessness, creativity, originality, spontaneity, trust, acceptance of self, others and nature, a democratic character structure, and an identification with humanity, all of which are aspects of an individual's self transcendence. I think we can reasonably also add a non-competitive character to the list of qualities.

To achieve full self-actualization, the needs of the first four levels must be met to a considerable extent, as they are a necessary foundation of support for these highest levels of human attainment. Self-actualization is the end goal, the "peak performance" of human development that we are working toward in our evolutionary education.

Competition and Non Competition in the Light of Maslow's Model

Maslow saw the needs of the first four levels as survival needs, with even love and esteem essential for optimum health. He also saw these needs as innate, a part of our genetic design. Like instincts, they drive (and explain) much of our behavior, and operate beneath the surface of our awareness. We don't go around consciously thinking, "Well, I'm no longer hungry or thirsty; now I'm going to start working on my safety needs." These stages happen organically; as each level of needs are sufficiently satisfied, we are naturally motivated to turn and focus on the next level.

Under stressful conditions, or when our survival is threatened, we often regress to a lower level. This kind of regression happened in the United States after the terrorist attacks of 2001. Before then, many Americans felt relatively secure in their surroundings. Now, at least on a subconscious level, many feel their safety and security threatened. Fear and insecurity spark a fight-or-flight tunnel vision that minimizes our critical faculties, distorts our perceptions of reality and makes us prone to irrational and aggressive/defensive behavior. This prevents us from developing our higher needs.

Research shows that a severe deficit during childhood in any of Maslow's first four levels may cause us to fixate on those needs for the rest of our lives. This is how Maslow understood neurosis. If we were poor, abused or abandoned, we may focus obsessively on these issues even if our circumstances greatly improve. Many people who experienced the poverty of the Great Depression continue to be frugal for the rest of their lives. Deficit thinking has become part of their cellular memory. Deprivation in the first four levels also triggers our lower survival instincts, making us more self-centered, competitive and aggressive or passive/aggressive in our efforts to get our needs met.

Maslow's model and insights explain much about the competitive culture in which we live, and why only a small fraction of the population – 2 % according to Maslow – achieves self-actualization. A competitively based system continually retriggers lower survival instincts that keep most people stuck in a continuous quest for the lower levels of needs in Maslow's hierarchy. Maslow's model also validates much of what I've presented here about non-competitive learning, which more naturally and effectively fosters development in the higher levels of Maslow's pyramid.

The primary goals and benefits of non-competitive learning include development of the practical, emotional and psychological skills that lead to proficiency, mastery and peak performance – which is another way to describe self-actualization. A non-competitive system would help everyone develop toward self-actualization. It would produce more self-actualized people in any population and society where it was applied, and also produce more self-actualized or enlightened societies. Every step we take toward a more cooperative learning model — a truly evolutionary educational system — hastens the arrival of this day.

ENLIGHTENED SELF-INTEREST

A competitive system is rooted in egoistic self-interest and operates in the lower levels of Maslow's pyramid. A cooperative system is rooted in enlightened self-interest and operates in the highest levels of Maslow's pyramid. Enlightened self-interest thrives and gets its own needs met at the highest levels while taking into consideration the needs of others and making sure they are also met.

I believe this book has shown why the shift from a competitive/ aggressive system to a non-competitive/cooperative system is both a matter of enlightened self-interest, and of urgent necessity. The evidence of my own experience and of my research in this field tells me two things: 1) We have reached a point in our evolution where the liabilities and dangers of the competitive model far outweigh the benefits. 2) A non-competitive model has enormous potential for our long-term growth and development in every area of human endeavor, from learning and business to social problems and politics. I believe this shift from a competitive to a cooperative model is essential to fulfilling our potential, individually and collectively, and also to our long-term survival as a species.

And in the End . . .

"Without love in the dream, it will never come true."

—Robert Hunter

In this book I have explored and revealed the darker aspects of a competitive system that, largely predicated on fear and scarcity, divides everyone into two narrow categories – a small fraction of winners and a majority of losers – who compete for prizes, money, prestige, and even survival. I've shown how the systematic and premature introduction of competition into the learning process subtly shifts our focus from learning and achieving proficiency in the fundamentals of a skill, to winning and losing; and how this skewed focus creates needless stress and inhibits the learning process. I've shown how competition stimulates and intensifies the fear of losing and the hope of winning into twin forces that drive our motivation and dominate our attention. I've shown how this distorts our values and character, encourages aggressive and unethical conduct, and interferes with the development of proficiency, excellence, mastery, and human potential.

I have also shown how Effortless Learning's non-competitive/ cooperative approach eliminates these negative aspects of the competitive system, greatly reducing stress and fostering deeper overall development of practical skills and all the qualities we associate with maturity, character and mastery. I've shown how Effortless Learning's dual focus on practical skill mastery and overall self-mastery facilitates our access to the zone, a state of consciousness beyond competition where we perform at our peak with seeming effortlessness. I have also demonstrated that in the right environment people can learn to play cooperatively together, with no desire to be competitive with each other, and can experience great joy in the process. For all these reasons, an Effortless Learning system facilitates our higher evolutionary development.

The cost of mastering any skill in any learning system is time, energy, dedication, and focused effort. But the competitive system magnifies the costs, limits the results and makes everyone adversaries in the process. It diminishes our energy, joy, creativity, mastery, and inhibits our access to the zone. A non-competitive system, where individuals cooperate with and support one another, generates more energy, joy, creativity and mastery. It facilitates our access to the zone, and makes it easier for a greater number of people to play "out of their minds". Since there is less stress in a non-competitive system it also gives us a new ability to relax and have the time to ponder the bigger questions of life.

Currently, competition is seen as the pinnacle or ultimate form of learning and functioning. As long as the competitive system dominates our educational process, we are each responsible for our own evolutionary education. As we educate ourselves in this non-competitive approach, it helps to join with other likeminded individuals until the system catches up. And as we reap the benefits of this approach, others *will* take notice and join in.

I believe that our competitive system has taken humankind as far as it can without destroying us. The state of the world today demonstrates the negative effects of a competitive system that is out of control. We see these effects in every aspect of human endeavor – education, sports, business, economics, politics, religion, interpersonal relations, and even in the decline of civility in public and private discourse. The nuclear arms race, the Cold War, the conflict between the West and Islam, the doctrine of Preemptive War, even global warming, all reflect the dark side of a competitive system that now threatens our survival as a species.

I believe a shift to non-competition and cooperation is now essential for our survival. And this can only be fully integrated into human culture through an educational system, based in these principles, that teaches and raises new generations of children with a more inclusive, cooperative and enlightened world-view. When we no longer see those around us as adversaries, great change is possible.

Maslow's Hierarchy of Needs, and his concept of Self-Actualization as the peak attainment of our human potential, points to non-competition/cooperation as the necessary next stage in man's evolutionary development. Remember that, according to Maslow, self-actualization cannot occur until our first four levels of needs – our physiological survival needs, our safety and security needs, our love and belonging needs, and our self-esteem needs – are significantly met. Before then, we live in recurring states of insecurity and fear, while these unmet needs dominate our attention and govern our behavior. Our aggressive/competitive nature and system grow out of these unmet needs, and also prevent their fulfillment.

Conscious competition represents a primitive phase of our evolution. It was an evolutionary step beyond primitive man's chaotic, fear-driven survival instinct, in that it provided a healthier and more creative focus for life than mere survival and the fear of death. The problem is that the competitive system forces us to compete endlessly against one another to meet our most basic needs in the first four tiers of Maslow's hierarchy. The competitive system doesn't lead to the fifth tier. By design, it creates a minority of winners and a vast majority of losers competing for insufficient rewards. This instills an ongoing tension in each of us as we vacillate between hope and fear, motivation and resignation in our efforts to meet our basic needs through competition.

This endless struggle is stressful, distracting, and makes it harder for most of us to get our basic needs met most of the time. It's a vicious cycle that keeps us struggling in the first four tiers, and prevents us from attaining the fifth tier – self-actualization.

According to Maslow, when the basic needs are met in the first four tiers, our stress level decreases, along with the urge to compete. We become aware of the higher needs of the fifth tier and begin to pursue them as we did the needs of the previous tiers. These fifth tier needs are spiritual; they include the desire for authenticity and cosmic meaning, to be our very best, to transcend our ego, and to achieve the fullness of our human potential.

Maslow's hierarchy of needs maps an evolutionary path out of our current competitive morass and all of the problems associated with it. He points to self-actualization as the ultimate goal of individual human life, and of human evolution. For a society to achieve this goal, its educational system must embrace, teach and reflect these evolutionary aims and values, which are non-competitive, and cooperative. And this is what Effortless Learning does. Evolutionary Education is true "higher education". It will create an evolution in human consciousness and usher in a more cooperative based society by raising a new generation of healthy, cooperative, non-competitive citizens who create a new and healthier world.

Everyone Has a Piece of the Puzzle

In another thought-provoking episode of *Star Trek: The Next Generation*, intelligent species from different galaxies learn of an ancient puzzle that, when put together, will reveal an extraordinary new power. Some believe this power will be an ultimate weapon capable of vanquishing all foes; some believe it will provide an unlimited energy source; and some believe it will yield the secrets of immortality. Each species desires this power and sets out in competition with the others to find the puzzle pieces and claim this ultimate power.

Eventually, each species has a piece of the puzzle, and they collectively find all the pieces – except for one. In the climax of the story they simultaneously converge on a planet where the last piece of the puzzle is located. There a conflict develops in which some species are ready to kill all the others to get their hands on this last piece, complete the puzzle, and control the mysterious new power.

Then the missing piece is found, and while the others are arguing, one of the humans puts the last piece in place, and activates the puzzle. A holographic image of an ancient being appears and tells them how, eons ago, his species traveled throughout the universe spreading the seeds of life on all of their home planets. Each of the species now gathered together, thinking they were separate from and superior to all the others, came from that ancient seeding. It turns out that they are all related to one another, originating from the same source, each one a piece of a puzzle, an essential part of a greater whole. They are not opponents, not enemies. The power they sought can only be found in unity and cooperation. This is the final message of the puzzle. This is its power. Competition was the last barrier to be overcome for the true puzzle to be solved.

This is the deeper lesson of Evolutionary Education that makes a competitive mentality a relic of the past. The reality, whether we wish to appreciate it or not, is that we are all on the same team. We live in an unfinished universe whose further development depends on our evolution. Our technological advances have made the world intimately interconnected. We now have unity in technology, but competition still dominates our consciousness. And this must change in order for us to fulfill our potential.

Evolutionary Education allows us to put the pieces of our own individual puzzle together and then add our piece to the greater whole. And it will allow us as a species to piece together the collective evolutionary puzzle we are all responsible for assembling. *Everyone* has a piece of the puzzle! If we leave anyone behind, the puzzle is incomplete.

In one of his last books, *The Descent of Man*, Charles Darwin concluded that the evolution of humankind succeeded not through the survival of the fittest, as he first thought, but through altruism and love, the essential glue that binds human beings together in family and community. This is the underlying idea that I hope this book will bring to light.

A common response to what I'm proposing is: "Everything you say sounds great, and I agree with you, but it will never happen." People who have been raised in a competitive system know only too well the myriad obstacles and forces that stand in the way of change. Resignation and pessimism have been programmed deeply into our collective cellular memory. But so have possibility and hope. Mankind's countless creations, discoveries and achievements in the forward march of our evolution tell us that the changes on which our future depends are possible.

Mathematician and philosopher Norbert Wiener, in his book The Human Use of Human Beings, states: "What gives our species its evolutionary edge is our vastly superior ability to change our behavior in response to feedback: changing information about the effectiveness or lack of effectiveness of past behavior and new information about present conditions. We have a further evolutionary advantage in that we can change our behavior quickly."

We humans are an amazing species, resilient, adaptable, with unlimited potential to imagine, create and accomplish our goals and dreams. In this book I have imagined a way of learning that also holds a key to a crucial decision confronting humanity: Will we move beyond our current aggressively competitive system into a more cooperative and peaceful future? And if so, how? I know that we have the potential and the ability; only time will tell if we have the wisdom and the resolve.

The shift from competition to cooperation involves a shift in our underlying philosophy, from pure self-interest to enlightened self-interest. Pure self-interest, with its short-term vision, seeks its own survival, regardless of the consequences to others, and often at the expense of others. And in doing so, it ultimately jeopardizes its own survival. Enlightened self-interest, with its long-term vision, takes the needs of others into consideration and works for the greater good, which includes its own long-term good, so that all may survive and thrive into the future.

Enlightened self-interest makes everyone's basic needs a top priority, while the competitive model makes the needs of the "lowest" level of humanity – the have-nots – the lowest priority. This failure of the majority of human beings to get their basic needs met keeps humanity stuck at its current level of evolution. Maslow showed that when individuals get their basic needs met, they naturally shift to their next evolutionary level. If we see humanity as one, we see that our collective evolutionary shift requires that the basic needs of a majority of humans must be met.

A system that helps everyone meet the needs of even the first two levels of Maslow's hierarchy will profoundly reduce societal and global stress and suffering, resulting in significant advances in every area of human endeavor for our entire species. Imagine the tremendous motivation and creativity that will be unleashed when we all feel safe, secure and fully alive, and perceive the richness and meaning of our existence. Imagine a global population of individuals living in states of self-actualization. Imagine the leap in human evolution!

It will take many people acting cooperatively to facilitate the necessary shift to a more cooperative paradigm. Fortunately, it won't require the agreement or cooperation of everyone on the planet;

maybe not even a majority. It will only require enough people to tip the scales, as Robert Axelrod's experiment with the "tit-for-tat strategy" showed.

These necessary changes in "humanity" are already happening, one individual at a time. When we begin to learn any skill in a non-competitive fashion, and incorporate this knowledge into every aspect of our lives, we become part of this greater evolution whether we know it or not. And as more and more Cooperators join our ranks, we shift the balance toward a more enlightened future.

You may say that I'm a dreamer,
but I'm not the only one.
I hope some day you'll join us,
and the world will live as one.
— John Lennon

Works Consulted

Introduction

Darwin, Charles. *On the Origin of Species*. E.P. Dutton. 1972.

Darwin, Charles. *On the Origin of Species*. E.P. Dutton. 1972.

Chapter 1

Eisler, Riane. *The Chalice & The Blade: Our History, Our Future*. Harper & Row. 1987

Darwin, Charles. *On the Origin of Species*. E.P. Dutton. 1972.

Sapolsky Robert, and Share, Lisa. *A Pacific Culture among Wild Baboons: Its Emergence and Transmission*. www.plosbiology. org. April 13, 2004

de Waal, Frans B.M. "Bonobo Sex and Society". *Scientific American*. March 1995

Margulis, Lynn. www.isepp.org/Pages/ San%20Jose%2004-05/ MargulisSaganSJ.html

May, Mark A. and Leonard Doob. *Cooperation and Competition*. Social Science Research Council. 1937.

Tutko, Thomas and Bruns, William. *Winning Is Everything and Other American Myths*. Macmillan. 1976.

Lipton, Bruce. *The Biology of Belief: Unleashing the Power of Consciousness, Matter and Miracles*. Mountain of Love/Elite Books. 2005

Human Genome Project. www.genomics.energy.gov

Kohn, Alfie. *No Contest: The Case Against Competition*. Houghton Mifflin. 1986.

Riesman, David. "Football in America: A Study in Culture Diffusion." Free Press. 1953.

CHAPTER 2

Kohn, Alfie. *No Contest: The Case Against Competition.* Houghton Mifflin. 1986.

Johnson, David W. and Roger T. Johnson. *Cooperation and Competition.* Interaction Book Co. 1989

McMurtry, John. *How Competition Goes Wrong.* Journal of Applied Science. 1991

Zimbardo, Phillip. *The Lucifer Effect: Understanding How Good People Turn Evil.* Random House 2007

CHAPTER 3

Gallwey W. Timothy. *Inner Tennis: Playing the Game.* Random House. 1976

Csikszentmihalyi, Mihaly. *Flow: The Psychology of Optimal Experience.* Harper & Row. 1990.

Kohn, Alfie. No Contest: The Case Against Competition. Houghton Mifflin. 1986.

Russell, David W. *Every Child An Achiever.* Kumon North America. 2002.

CHAPTER 4

Johnson, David W. and Roger T. Johnson. *Cooperation and Competition.* Interaction Book Co. 1989.

Kohn, Alfie. *No Contest: The Case Against Competition.* Houghton Mifflin. 1986.

Miller, Alice. *For Your Own Good.* Farrar, Straus, Giroux. 2002

Chapter 5

Lipton, Bruce. *The Biology of Belief: Unleashing the Power of Consciousness, Matter and Miracles*. Mountain of Love/ Elite Books. 2005

Loehr, James. *Mental Toughness Training for Sports: Achieving Athletic Excellence*. M. Evans and Co. 1986

Huizinga, Johan. *Homo Ludens: A Study of the Play Elements in Culture*. Maurice Temple Smith Ltd., 1970.

Chapter 7

Axelrod, Robert. *The Evolution of Cooperation*. Basic. 1984.

Robert Kurzban & Daniel Houser. *The Economist*, January 22, 2005

Hamm, Steve. "LinuxInc." *Business Week*, January 31, 2005

Chapter 8

Ansbacher, Heinz L. and Ansbacher, Rowena R. *The Individual Psychology of Alfred Adler*. Basic Books 1956

Maslow, Abraham. Dr. C. George Boeree, www.ship.edu

And In The End...

Darwin, Charles. *The Descent of Man*. The Werner Company.

Recommended Reading & Resources

Richard Bach- *Jonathan Livingston Seagull, Illusions, One*

Ernest Callenbach-*Ecotopia*

Carlos Castaneda-all his books, *The Teaching's of Don Juan "A Yaqui Way of Knowledge", A Separate Reality, Journey to Ixtlan*

Deepak Chopra-*How to Know God*

Ram Dass-*Be Here Now, The Only Dance There Is, More Grist For The Mill*

Riane Eisler-*The Chalice and the Blade*

Marilyn Ferguson-*The Aquarian Conspiracy*

Rick Fields-*Chop Wood Carry Water*

Robert Fritz-*The Path of Least Resistance*

Paulo Freire-*Pedagogy of the Oppressed, Education for Critical Consciousness*

Tim Gallwey-*Inner Tennis "Playing the Game"*

Malcolm Gladwell-*The Tipping Point: How Little Things Can Make a Big Difference*

Thich Nhat Hanh-*Being Peace*

Ken Keyes-*Handbook to Higher Consciousness*

Alfie Kohn-*No Contest: The Case Against Competition, Punished By Rewards: In Search of A's, Praise, Incentive Plans, and other Bribes.*

Dan Millman-*Way of the Peaceful Warrior, Body Mind Mastery, The Life You Were Born to Live, No Ordinary Moments, Laws of Spirit*

Robert Ornstein-*The Evolution of Consciousness*

M. Scott Peck-*The Road Less Traveled*

Ayn Rand-*Atlas Shrugged, The Fountainhead*

James Redfield-*The Celestine Prophesy*

Tom Robbins-*Even Cowgirls Get The Blues, Another Roadside Attraction, Still Life With Woodpecker, Jitterbug Perfume*

Jane Roberts- all the Seth books- *Seth Speaks, The Nature of Personality, The Individual and the Nature of Mass Events*

John-Roger & Peter McWilliams-*Life 101*

Don Miguel Ruiz-*The Four Agreements, The Voice of Knowledge*

Bill & Win Sweet-*Living Joyfully With Children*

Neal Donald Walsch-Conversations with God, Books 1, 2, & 3

Tom Wolfe-*The Electric Koolaid Acid Test*

RESOURCES

TaKeTiNa-Rhythm for Evolution-www.taketina.com

HeartMath-www.hearthmath.com

Index

About the Author

Brent Zeller has seen the competitive system "up close and personal," having spent most of his life immersed in the highly competitive and challenging sport of tennis. For four decades, Brent has devoted his life to the study of the learning process, and of that fable state called "the zone." He has done extensive research as a student, a teacher, an athlete, a musician, and through the study of philosophy, psychology, current events, and history.

Brent graduated from the College of William & Mary with a B.S. in Geology in 1976. He played tournament tennis for eighteen years, attaining rankings locally, statewide, and regionally. As a tennis teacher since 1974, Brent has worked with thousands of people, logging over 20,000 hours of on court observation. Since 1992, through his non-competitive tennis program, Effortless Tennis, he has taught students how to enjoy playing tennis without having to compete, and, if it is their desire, how to succeed in a competitive environment. He has been a member of the United States Professional Tennis Association since 1975. Articles on "the zone" and non-competitive learning have appeared in the San Francisco Chronicle, The Marin Independent Journal, Inside Tennis Magazine, The Point Reyes Light, and various Internet websites. Brent's thirty-five years of teaching experience and his observations of the world around him led to the conclusions revealed in this book.

CPSIA information can be obtained at www.ICGtesting.com

2239511.V00001B/6/P

9 781595 943095